Creative
Home Decorations
You Can Make

Creative
Home Decorations
You Can Make

Low-cost Ways to Beautify Your Home

By Karen Carlson McCann

With Sue T. Garmon

Drawings and photographs
by Karen Carlson McCann

AVENEL BOOKS • NEW YORK

To my husband, Stephen,
who puts up with all of
my projects

K. C. McC.

Contents

Introduction

Much has been said about the bored American housewife. It's true that cleaning, cooking and ironing aren't always stimulating, but there are many creative things a woman can do in her spare minutes to break the monotony of a daily routine.

You may say, "I don't have any spare time," but you'll be surprised how much extra time you can find when you're doing something you enjoy.

The biggest problem seems to be that most women don't really know where or how to begin, especially if they feel they have no artistic ability. Paints, hammers and saws are foreign objects and throw most women into a state of panic. However, with a few basic directions and guides, a trip to the paint store or the lumber yard won't be such a frustrating experience.

This book is full of creative ideas that can be completed in a short time by those who desire to beautify their homes, make gifts for friends, or preserve their sanity. Anyone, man or woman, derives a great deal of satisfaction from creating something beautiful with his own hands.

Many of the items you can make by following the instructions in this book are sold in boutique shops for as much as three or four times the cost of making them. But if you buy one, you don't get the satisfaction of smiling and saying, "I made it."

You may already have the materials needed for many of the creative crafts in this book; and if not, they are not expensive.

One word of advice: once you get "hooked" on making these things it's tempting to let your other responsibilities slide. So it's a good idea to get the housework done first and then get busy on your projects. You'll find it will even make housework easier because you'll hurry through your chores looking forward to doing something you enjoy.

After trying a few of these ideas you'll be surprised to find how imaginative you really are. Soon your creative instincts will provide you with new ideas of your own.

Creative
Home Decorations
You Can Make

1. The Gentle Art of Home Decoration

The purpose of interior decoration should be to make your home not only beautiful but comfortable and easy to live in. Remember when planning a job of decorating that your home doesn't have to look like a magazine advertisement. All it has to do is please you—you live in it!

Whether they know it or not, most women have a knack for decoration. Any woman who can follow a simple recipe can be a successful decorator.

Here's the magic formula:

Take lots of love
Mix well with a spoonful of hospitality
Add an extravagant dollop of personality

Season with:

A dash of color
A pinch of spice
A touch of genius
A heap of imagination

Blend it all together, let it simmer, and the results will astound you!

A Dash of Color
(Color and Color Co-ordinates)

There are no difficult and complicated rules to follow in choosing colors for your home. The only really important factor to be considered is your personal taste. Don't shy away from experimenting with color and color combinations. If you like a color, use it!

Combine colors which seem to have an affinity for each other. If you feel that they naturally belong together, they probably do. Or if you think they're not naturally compatible, but have a vague idea that they'd harmonize or offer a striking contrast, go ahead and try them. Most colors will blend together easily enough if you're careful to choose the proper shades and tints. You'll see that Mother Nature has no problems blending colors, her range is as wide as creation; so take a tip from her!

17

Let color create a mood for you. Use it to give a room an air of soothing harmony, warm interest, or intense excitement. Muted shades of blues, greens and lavenders have a cool, refreshing look and are most welcome in bedroom areas, or other places reserved for quiet thought. Sunshine colors, such as orange, yellow and red have a stimulating effect, and can be used to great advantage in the breakfast nook or kitchen— where they'll provide a cheery note on dreary, dismal winter mornings. You can tone down a wide-awake room, subdue a boisterous one with muted shades used as accent colors, or bring a drab and lusterless room to life with splashes of unexpected, vivid hues.

The thing to keep in mind when selecting your colors is simply this: color is like any other seasoning. Too much makes a dish overpowering, while too little makes it. bland and tasteless.

A Pinch of Spice
(Fabrics and Textures)

Few of us give a second thought to choosing a deliberate variety of fabrics, so long as the colors are suitable for our purposes. Yet fabrics and textures, like color, can be used to relieve monotony and add zest and flavor to a decorative scheme. By a careful blending of assorted fabrics and textures you can establish a mood of bold excitement, flirtatious femininity, or pleasing serenity. In choosing your fabrics, base your selection upon the mood you wish to create.

Use rough, nubby weaves with the texture of straw, wicker, or bamboo for a casual, informal, and highly contemporary look. This combination goes well anywhere, has a satisfyingly modern appearance, and can savor slightly of the exotic if you choose.

Delicate fabrics with fine, wispy textures give a room a look of dainty femininity. Unless your home is a strictly feminine one, however, these fabrics aren't recommended for general use throughout your home. No man would be happy for any length of time in a house smothered in chiffon!

Silky and velvetlike fabrics, combined with the texture of highly polished wood, create an atmosphere of sophisticated elegance. The resultant rich, dramatic effect blends well with a traditional, classic decor.

When selecting your fabrics, try to co-ordinate them with the rest of your home. If, for example, its present look is airy and contemporary, don't go all-out for silk or velvet. If your fabrics and textures are carefully chosen to blend in with what you already have, you'll find they produce a picture of harmony and well-established order, always desirable in any home.

One note of warning: be very cautious when mixing fabric patterns in a room. Lush floral prints, zebra stripes and highland plaids just DON'T belong together. Taken separately, each pattern can provide a charming accent; together, they form an eyesore. So if you've more than one of these patterns in any one room, either recover the furniture, or move a couple of pieces to different rooms to avoid undesirable clashes.

Choose your fabrics for interest and eye appeal, but look for those which will flatter, complement and complete the picture in your mind.

Take your time in making your selections—you will have to live with your decisions a long time.

A Touch of Genius
(Furniture and Its Arrangement)

Every woman is born with a touch of genius—sometimes called feminine intuition. So go right ahead and let it work for you in selecting and arranging your furniture. Of course, it's nice if you can start from scratch with all new furnishings, but let's face it—for most of us this idea is so impractical as to be slightly ridiculous. Use your native thrift and American know-how to do the best you can with what you already have. You'll find it rewarding and a lot of fun.

Often a little rearranging of furniture, or perhaps adding a piece or two, is just what a room needs to give it a lift. This may mean moving pieces from one room to another, and for a while this may cause a bit of confusion. But once the family gets used to the change, they'll stop stumbling over it in the night.

If a couple of pieces seem to stick out like a sore thumb despite your best efforts, it might be worth your while to try refinishing them. With just a little effort, they might turn out to be your prize possessions!

Generally, the essential thing to strive for in every room is a feeling of balance and an uncluttered look. Just a glance will sometimes tell you if the arrangement is a happy one. If you're not sure, try adding and/or removing one or two pieces of furniture, stand back, and see what effect you've achieved by doing so. It may take a little time to produce the desired effect, but eventually, with a bit of patient handling, your pieces will fall into the proper pattern.

You don't have to be a connoisseur of furniture styles and periods to work with and select furniture for your home. The important thing is that YOU like and will enjoy what you choose. If this means a mixing and blending of various styles, don't be afraid to try it. Just keep it comfortable, and everyone will be happy!

A Heap of Imagination
(The Use of "Decorator" Accessories You Made)

Imagination—listed here last—is the basic ingredient necessary to create anything, whether it be an artistic masterpiece, a literary or musical composition, a space satellite or a home.

The funny thing about imagination is that the more you use it, the more of it you have to use. It replenishes itself, and one idea seems to generate another.

In this book you will be given an assortment of unusual ideas for creating objects to decorate your home. By the time you're finished your imagination, like the green bay tree, should be flourishing.

So put it to work!

And if some of your more imaginative schemes for decoration seem a bit far-fetched, just ask yourself: Where would we be today if Columbus hadn't had the courage of his convictions?

2. A Woman's Basic Workshop

Most men think of a woman's workshop as consisting of such items as manicure scissors, nail files, emery boards, eyelash curlers, brush rollers, hair spray and razor blades (his).

For these projects, however, there are a few additional basic items you should have handy. You needn't buy the most expensive tools, but the cheapest won't last long, so stay in the middle of the road. After you start working, you may want to add to this list, and for some projects you'll need special materials. This is simply a list of the things most commonly used, most of which can be found in your local hardware or dime store. Don't panic if you don't know how to use these tools! After a few good hacks and whacks, it'll be a snap.

For the real novice, a drawing of each tool will help you recognize it (although I hope that's not necessary).

Basic Equipment

TOOLS

Hammer

Pliers

Screwdriver

Wire Cutters

23

Saw

Small Drill

Utility Knife
This has a heavy metal
handle with replaceable blades

Scissors

You'll soon learn to improvise, using other everyday household objects such as tweezers, ice picks and old toothbrushes.

Other Equipment

assortment of nails and screws
white glue
epoxy glue, sometimes called iron glue
sandpaper—medium, fine, and very fine grades
steel wool—triple 0 grade
flexible wire
heavy string
paint brushes—varying in width from fine to 1½ inches. Be sure to get real bristle brushes. They last longer
ruler
yardstick
measuring tape

mixing pans—pot pie and frozen pie tins are ideal for this purpose
turpentine
newspaper—invaluable for protecting your tables and floors from paint and paste
tin cans
thumb tacks and pins
tongue depressors or wooden picnic spoons—these may be used for mixing paint and then thrown away
paper towels—great for cleaning up and many other purposes
lacquer thinner

Storage and Care of Supplies and Equipment

Shoe boxes or cigar boxes are excellent containers for storing your supplies so they are easy to find and use. Label each box with a felt pen (Magic Marker) so you'll know what it contains.

Paint brushes should always be kept standing on the handles. Never leave them standing on the bristles, as this ruins the brush. An empty coffee can is a fine paint brush holder.

Brushes should be cleaned thoroughly after each use. Be sure to read the instructions on the paint can to see whether you should use turpentine or lacquer thinner for cleaning, and then pour a little into a tin can. Slosh your brush around a bit to remove all the paint, then wipe it on some newspaper.

To finish cleaning your brush, scrub it on a bar of naphtha soap under running warm water, rinse the brush thoroughly, and it's ready to use again.

The Work Area

Ideally, you should have a separate room in which to work. Usually, however, this is not practical; so settle for an out-of-the-way corner where you can set up shop. In general, the work area should be warm, uncramped, well lighted, and as dust-free as possible. Specifically, you will need a table to work on and a cupboard or shelves for storing your supplies and equipment. The bigger the table the better, although a card table or folding table can be used.

Your work will be easier and more fun if your shop is well organized.

Shopping Sources for Supplies and Equipment

adhesive picture hanger
  dime store
air conditioner filter
  hardware store
ball fringe
  dime store or fabric shop
balloons
  dime store
book ends (metal or wooden)
  dime store
box, wooden
  hobby shop

braid (silver, gold, etc. for trimming)
  dime store or yard goods store
brass rings (2 with chain)
  hardware store
bulletin board
  dime store
burlap
  yard goods store
buttons
  dime store
cafe-curtain rings and rods
  hardware or dime store
candle
  dime or department store
candleholders (glass)
  dime store
candleholding bracket (metal)
  some hardware stores (a metal bottle cover may be used instead)
canister
  dime store
cardboard
  dime store or hobby shop
chicken wire
  lumber yard or hardware store
clay (moist, self-hardening)
  hobby shop or art store; usually sold in 5-lb. packages
colander (metal)
  dime store
crepe paper
  dime store
doughnut cutters
  hardware or dime store
doweling
  hardware store
drinking straws (plastic)
  supermarket or dime store
duck decoy
  sporting goods shop
Duco cement
  hardware or dime store

enamel (hobby, in ¼-oz. bottles)
dime store or hobby shop

epoxy glue
hardware store or hobby shop

felt (10-inch squares)
dime store or yard goods store

figurines (plaster)
dime store

file (cardboard, accordion-type)
business supply store; dime store;
some department stores

filter (for air conditioner)
hardware store

florist clay
dime store

florist tape
dime store or florist shop

flowerpot (clay)
dime store

footstool
department store; some dime
stores

frame (finished or unfinished)
dime store

fringe or braid
dime store or yard goods store

gold braid
dime store or yard goods store

gold paint
hardware or dime store

grout (for work with mosaic tiles)
hobby shop; tile company or hardware store

hat rack (expandable, wooden)
hardware or dime store

ice tongs (old-fashioned, iron)
your attic; antique store; junk shop

India ink
dime store or art store

individual metal molds for gelatin
desserts and salads
dime store

lace
yard goods store or dime store

letter holder
dime store

mat board
art store

molding
lumber yard or hardware store

mosaic tiles and cement
hobby shop or tile company

net
dime store or yard goods store

nut cups (paper or cardboard)
dime store

nuts (in the shell)
grocery store or supermarket

paint
hardware; dime or paint store

paper (heavy white writing or art)
dime store or art supply shop

picture hangers
dime store

picture-hanging bracket
hardware or dime store

pin clasps
hobby shop

plastic flowers
dime store

fruit
dime store

leaves
dime store

spray
hardware or paint store

plates
dime store

poster board
dime store

ribbon
dime store

rickrack or braid
dime store or yard goods store

roller (*wooden*)
paint or wall paper stores

salt and pepper shakers (*metal*)
dime store

scraper and cement spreader
hobby shop or tile company

screen (*partitioned*)
department store; some lumber yards and hardware stores

sequin pins
dime store or yard goods store

sequins
dime store or hobby shop

shelf brackets (*metal*)
hardware store

shower curtain liner
dime store

solder, liquid
hardware store

spray paint
hardware or paint store

steel wool
hardware store

styrofoam (*balls, cones, rings, etc.*)
hobby shop or florist shop

table legs (*in kit, with brackets*)
hardware store

tray (*metal or wooden*)
dime store

Treasure Gold Wax Gilt
hobby shop; hardware store or art store

trimmings (*braid, rickrack, lace*)
dime store; yard goods store or department store

upholstery tacks
hardware or dime store

utility knife
hardware store

wallpaper paste
paint or hardware store

watering can (*metal or plastic*)
hardware or dime store

wire
hardware store

wood
lumber yard

wooden appliqués
some hardware stores and lumber companies

yardstick
paint stores usually give these away

yarn
dime store

3. Wall Decorations

Unusual wall decorations fill empty spaces, brighten dull corners, and add color to any room. Let them reflect your own life and personality!

Framing and Displaying Photographs

Don't hide your prize snapshots in a photo album. Show them off!

Here's a simple but effective way to put your favorite people and places on display.

MATERIALS NEEDED

snapshots—colored or black and white

frame—you can buy one already finished, or stain an unfinished frame (see pages 39–40, this chapter). Your frame should be 18 × 24 inches or larger, depending upon how many pictures you want to display.

glass—the size of your frame

2 pieces of heavy cardboard—same size as the glass

gold braid—1 yard each of five or six different designs.

colored burlap—2 inches larger on each side than the cardboard.

½-inch brass straight pins

white glue

masking tape

DIRECTIONS

Cover the front of one piece of cardboard with white glue. If you don't want to be coated with glue up to your elbows, squeeze out some glue, take a paper towel, dip it in a dish of water, and use this to smooth out the glue.

Cover the cardboard with the burlap. Glue the overlapping material onto the back of the cardboard.

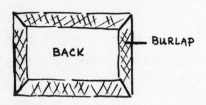

Let this dry, and don't worry if the glue seeps through your material; just wipe off the worst of it. The rest will dry and won't show.

Arrange your photographs on the material, varying the sizes and shapes of your pictures for a pleasing effect.

Pin each picture in place by pushing a pin through the corner of the picture and the cardboard. Bend the pin point up even with the back of the cardboard so it won't stick out.

Trim the edges of each snapshot with gold braid, securing it in place with pins. (The pictures can be changed periodically if you wish.)

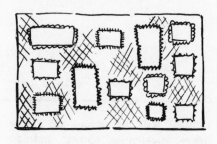

Place your glass in the frame, then the cardboard with the pictures, and put in the remaining piece of cardboard.

Overlap masking tape around the edges where the cardboard and frame meet to keep the contents intact.

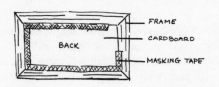

Wooden Wall Plaques

Decorative wooden plaques are marvelous for your children's room, the kitchen, or to hang with a picture arrangement in your living room. They're guaranteed to cause a flurry of admiring comments.

A handsaw can be used to cut the various shapes, but it's easier to find a friend with a jig saw, catch him in a weak moment, and talk him into cutting them for you.

MATERIALS NEEDED

pine boards—1 inch thick by 12 inches wide. The length depends upon how many plaques you want to make. Allow about 18 inches for each

handsaw
sandpaper—medium, fine, and very fine grades
wood stain or semi-gloss enamel
small tubes of oil paints—three or four colors to complement the color scheme of your room
paint brush
turpentine
satin finish varnish
picture hangers

DIRECTIONS

Draw a simple outline design on plain paper or cardboard, staying within the size limitations of your wood. You don't need to be an artist, just go ahead and try!

Here are a few shapes you might enlarge and try, although there is a great variety of designs you can use.

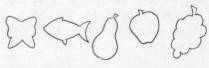

When you have a drawing which satisfies you, cut it out, place it on the wood, and trace around the edges.

Saw around the outline drawing.

Starting with a medium-grade sandpaper, begin sanding your plaque to smooth it, and round the edges. When you've taken off the roughest part, switch to fine, then to very fine sandpaper. Don't give up until it's perfectly satiny to the touch. The secret of a professional job is in the sanding—the smoother it is, the better the finished product will be. The trick in sanding is to make sure to rub in the same direction as the grain of the wood.

When you've finished sanding, be sure all sawdust has been brushed or wiped off so the surface is perfectly clean. It is also important to remove every speck of sawdust from your work area, as the whole project can be ruined if any sawdust lands on the paint while it is still wet.

At this point you must make a decision. You may paint your plaque either with a semi-gloss enamel in a color of your choice, or you may stain it. The choice will depend upon the room in which you wish to display it.

If you choose to paint it with enamel, use two coats, letting it dry thoroughly between coats.

To stain the plaque, choose a stain that will match your furniture: walnut, maple, fruitwood, etc. Apply two coats of stain with a rag, being sure to wipe off any excess with a clean rag so the color will be even. Let your paint or stain dry overnight.

With a pencil, lightly draw geometric shapes on your plaque. Then paint these with oils, using three or four different colors.

When the paints are completely dry, give each plaque two coats of varnish.

Nail the picture hanger into place, attach your plaque.

Burlap Wall Hangings

Wall hangings can provide a vivid splash of color. They're easy enough for the whole family to work on, and they can be fashioned from various odds and ends you may have in the house.

There is a never-ending variety of designs to use: a big Santa for Christmas, a Thanksgiving scene, bright flowers, seascapes, or animals—you

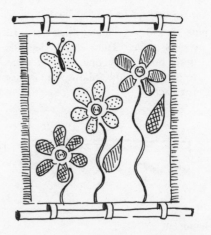

might even try a comic strip character! Just let your imagination be your guide.

colored burlap—decide what size and color hanging would look best on your wall

scraps of material left over from sewing, felt, string, ribbon and rickrack

buttons

white glue

2 pieces of doweling—each 3 inches longer than your picture and ½ inch in diameter

pinking shears——your sewing basket.

DIRECTIONS

Cut your burlap to the desired size, leaving an extra inch on the top and bottom for a hem. Turn back the hem, which may be sewed or glued into place, and fringe the two outside edges.

Next, draw a simple pattern. Shelf paper is inexpensive and useful for this purpose. However, if you prefer, use a picture from a child's coloring book to cut apart as your pattern.

Now it's time to put your imagination to work. Trace and cut your picture from various brightly colored materials. Be sure to use pinking shears for cutting. It looks better, and the edges won't fray.

Glue each piece securely into place. Add details and decorations to your picture with buttons, string, rickrack, yarn, etc.

For example, the picture shown here could be made by cutting the sails, boat and clouds from several bright prints. Trim the sails and boat with yarn and string, buttons for portholes, and rickrack for the water.

To complete the picture for hanging, you will need six 4-inch pieces of ribbon. Fold each piece in half to make a loop and sew to the back hem on the top and bottom. Slip the doweling, which may be painted, through the loops.

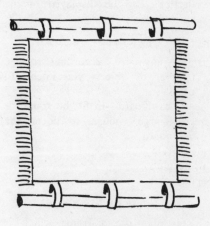

Displaying Family Mementos

Dig out those old Boy Scout pins, Girl Scout pins, high school awards or medals, sorority or fraternity pins, and old watches which have been hidden for years in your overcrowded dresser drawers. Believe it or not,

they make individual and different wall decorations. Shell, rock and coin collections can be displayed in the same manner.

MATERIALS NEEDED

frame—any size, according to the number of objects you intend to use
heavy cardboard—to fit the frame
velvet—large enough to cover the cardboard
gold braid
white glue
epoxy glue

DIRECTIONS

You may use a frame which is already finished, but it's a lot more fun and much less expensive to finish your own (see Picture Framing section).

Completely cover one side of the cardboard with white glue. Be sure to spread the glue with paper towels dipped in a little water. This saves your fingers and spreads the glue evenly.

Cover the cardboard with velvet material, stretching it slightly as you glue it down to avoid making wrinkles.

When the glue has dried, arrange and attach your mementos to the velvet. Those which already have pin backs, such as sorority or fraternity pins, can be mounted as they are. Others, such as watches or medals, with metal loops on top, can be held in place with fancy hat pins. Use epoxy glue to secure any objects that cannot be pinned to the velvet.

Place the cardboard in the frame, using masking tape around the back

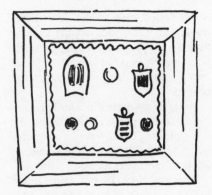

to hold the cardboard and frame tightly together.

For a finishing touch, trim the outside edges of the velvet with gold braid.

Decoupage or Antique Pictures

You needn't spend a fortune for custom-built frames to preserve and display intriguing pictures and maps. Decoupage, a unique method which was first used centuries ago, permits you to exhibit things without frames.

Any type of picture may be used if it is prepared correctly. Magazines, post cards, greeting cards and calendars are excellent sources for finding pictures.

Don't be alarmed by the complexity

of the directions. It's much easier than it sounds. Work carefully, step by step, and you'll be amazed by the finished product. While you have all the materials ready for use, it's a good idea to do a group of pictures rather than just one; it doesn't take much longer.

Note: These same directions may be used to decoupage many other articles such as wooden boxes, wastebaskets or trays.

MATERIALS NEEDED

wood—plywood works well and is fairly inexpensive, but any type of wood may be used. It must be at least ½ inch thick

sandpaper—fine and very fine grades

plastic spray

steel wool—triple 0 grade—or a very fine grade

flat black enamel spray—this is needed *only* if the picture has printing on the back of it

small wooden roller (seam roller)

wood stain or semi-gloss enamel—any color which will be a suitable background for your picture

The finishing coats should be done with one of the following paints, depending upon whether you used stain or enamel to color your wood

Sherwin-Williams Mar-Not Satin Varnish—for boards painted with enamel

Deft Clear Bar Top Finish—for stained boards.

tack rag—you will find this at a hardware or paint store

paste wax

white glue

velvet ribbon—¼ inch wide, and long enough to go around the perimeter of your board

There are many devices for hanging pictures, all of which can be found in a hardware or dime store

picture-hanging bracket

or, brass ring

or, hooks with picture wire

DIRECTIONS

The wood should be cut to the correct size. Many lumber yards will do this for a slight fee, and you'll find it's worth the added cost if you don't have a knack for wood cutting.

The board, when cut, should be at least one inch wider on each side than the picture you've selected.

Sand the board, first with fine sandpaper and then very fine, until it's perfectly smooth. Don't forget the edges.

Finish the board with two coats of a wood stain or semi-gloss enamel.

Prepare the picture for mounting while the paint is drying. If there is any printing or writing on the back of the picture, spray it with a flat black enamel. This will prevent it from showing through.

Cut out the picture carefully, removing any unnecessary borders or margins. For a more antique look, the edges may be neatly torn rather than cut.

Spray both sides of the picture with two coats of plastic spray. This will prevent the colors from running or fading.

Now comes the sticky part! Squeeze white glue all over the picture back, spreading it with paper towels dipped in a little water. It's better to use too much glue than not enough. Any surplus can always be wiped off with a damp towel. Every bit of paper *must* be well covered with glue.

Place the picture squarely on the board, smoothing it carefully from the center out with a damp paper towel. Then, using the wooden roller, roll firmly over the picture, again working from the center, until all excess glue and air bubbles have been forced out.

When the glue is dry, wipe the board thoroughly with a tack rag to remove any lint or dust, and apply your first coat of Mar-Not or Deft. Continue applying coats of Deft or Mar-Not until you can no longer feel the edge of the picture. This will take from fifteen to forty coats. Each layer must be completely dry before the second one may be applied. Be sure to wipe the board and picture carefully with a tack rag before each painting, as lint or dust will produce bubbles. After every fourth or fifth coat, rub over the entire decoupage with the steel wool to remove any unwanted lumps or bumps. Finally, rub lightly with steel wool and follow with a coat of good paste wax.

Trim the outside edge of the board with velvet ribbon and attach your selection of picture hanger.

Picture Framing

No man ever thinks any woman can hang a picture straight, much less frame one. So let's see if we can't prove him wrong.

The following are the five main parts used to frame a picture, with directions and suggestions for putting it all together.

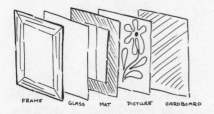

FRAME GLASS MAT PICTURE CARDBOARD

The Frame

Starting with an unfinished frame from the dime store, hardware or department store, you can finish it in a number of ways. Some techniques are very simple, others more elaborate.

PREPARATIONS

If there are any dents or scratches in the wood, hold a wet sponge over them until the dents swell back into place. Next, sand the frame, using very fine sandpaper, until it's very smooth.

From this point on there are many ways to complete the frame.

If you like the look of raw wood, just apply five or six coats of a good paste *wax*, letting it dry twenty-four hours between coats.

To *stain* the frame, use two coats of a good wood stain. Follow that with two coats of a satin finish varnish and a coat of paste wax.

Pictures for the children's room or kitchen look saucy and gay in frames *painted* with brightly colored gloss or semi-gloss enamel.

Another simple way to finish a frame is to rub it with *wax shoe polish* of any color. Let the polish dry, then shine it with a clean rag.

To make an *antique* frame, first paint it with a flat or semi-gloss enamel and let it dry thoroughly. Make an antique glaze by mixing a contrasting color of tube oil paint with an equal amount of turpentine. Dip a clean rag into the glaze and apply to the frame, wiping more into the corners and grooves. Let it set for about five minutes. Then, using a clean textured cloth, such as cheesecloth or terry cloth, wipe away some of the glaze, creating highlights. (For a more complete description of antiquing, see Chapter 8, pages 119–20.) To achieve a wormhole effect (optional), follow the directions for antiquing until the glaze is dry. Then dip a small brush or toothbrush into black or dark brown enamel or oil paint and flick small droplets onto the frame. Finish your antique frame with a coat of flat or semi-gloss varnish. For a very lavish effect, apply Treasure Gold, or a liquid gold leaf to various parts of the frame after the coat of varnish has dried.

The Glass

Many frames come already equipped with their own glass. However, if your frame does not have glass, most hardware stores or glass companies will cut a piece to fit your frame. Non-glare glass is usually most satisfactory for framing pictures, but it adds quite a bit to the expense. Some types of paintings, such as oils and some tempera paintings which have been varnished, need no glass covering.

The Mat

It's not necessary to mat all pictures. Oil paintings are never matted. As a general rule, however, most other paintings should be matted.

Mat board may be bought at any art supply store and comes in a variety of colors, bright and subtle. Choose a shade which will complement the picture you're framing and the wall on which it will hang.

Cut the mat board the same size as the glass by drawing a utility knife along the edge of a metal ruler or yardstick. The inside of the mat should be cut in the same manner. Matting board is fairly thick and a little hard to cut, so two extra hands are extremely helpful to keep the ruler from slipping.

The mat may be of any width, but generally the bigger the picture, the wider the mat.

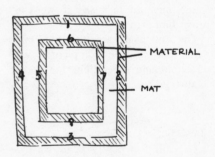

For a very unusual effect, cover the mat with linen, burlap or velvet material.

The material should be cut at least 1 inch larger (on all eight sides) than the mat.

Snip the corners of the material up to the edges of the mat.

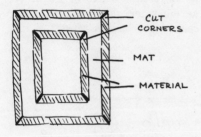

Then simply overlap the material onto the back of the board, holding it in place with glue or masking tape.

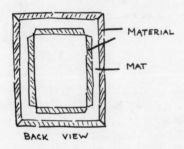

BACK VIEW

The Picture

The picture should be cut to overlap the mat by at least ½ inch, and held securely in place with masking tape.

The Cardboard Backing

Heavy cardboard backing is used to protect and hold everything together, and it should be cut to the same dimensions as the glass. This is held firmly in place by overlapping the cardboard and frame with wide masking tape.

Simulated Silk Screens

For an illusion of richness or some color excitement in a blandly furnished room or a distressingly empty corner, add one of these luxurious screens, and you will create a focal point of interest, stamped with your own personality.

Unlike real silk screens, these are remarkably easy to make, and they are just as effective as the genuine article. Don't be surprised if your friends ask for duplicates!

MATERIALS NEEDED

heavy cotton fabric—of a solid color to be used as the background. A half-yard makes a good-sized hanging, but it may be made larger by using more fabric

2 cafe-curtain rods—each rod should be at least 2 inches longer than the finished picture

cafe-curtain rings—10 or more

4 pieces of heavy paper—each piece should be the same size as your fabric background. Heavy brown wrapping paper or butcher paper may be used

flat enamel spray—3 different colors of your choice

iron
scissors
pencil
carbon paper—1 package, any size
masking tape
needle
thread—to match the fabric background

DIRECTIONS

Iron the fabric to remove all folds and wrinkles, and cut it to the size you intend to make the hanging. Allow for a half-inch hem on all four sides.

Use tiny stitches to sew the hem, and iron it neatly when you've finished.

Cut four pieces of heavy paper the same size as the fabric.

Decide upon a design. There is a wide range of subjects from which to choose; birds, animals, flowers, boats, or imaginative abstract shapes. Doodle on a small piece of scratch paper until you come up with a satisfactory picture. Keep your drawing *very* simple with no small details, and it will be much easier to transfer to the cloth.

Using one piece of the heavy paper, carefully enlarge the picture you've selected. Be sure to make each object the exact size and shape you want it

ENLARGE PICTURE

to be on the final wall hanging. You now have your pattern to work from.

Decide what color you would like to make each object or shape. Keep in mind the three colors of spray enamel you have selected.

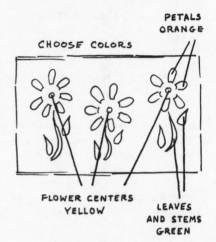

A separate stencil must be made for applying each color to the fabric background. (For three colors you will need three stencils.)

To make one stencil, place another piece of heavy paper on the table, carbon paper on top of that, and your pattern on top of the carbon paper.

Trace around all of the objects you want to make one color; for example, trace everything which is to be painted orange.

Remove the pattern and carbon paper and cut around the outline of each object on the stencil. Discard the pieces you cut out, as you will not need them. The piece of paper with the holes in it is your stencil. When paint is sprayed on the stencil, it will go through the holes onto the fabric background.

TRACE AROUND ALL
ORANGE OBJECTS

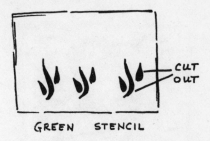

GREEN STENCIL

Place one stencil on top of the fabric, being sure the corners and sides are straight and even. Use several pieces of masking tape to hold the fabric and stencil to the newspaper so they will not slip or slide while you're spray-painting.

Spray the paint onto the stencil. Fill the holes completely with paint.

Remove the stencil and let the paint dry for twenty-four hours.

Then attach the second stencil in the same way, spray it with another color, and let this one dry.

Follow with your third stencil and color.

After the last has dried, attach the cafe-curtain rings to the top and bottom of your creation, and slip the curtain rods into the rings.

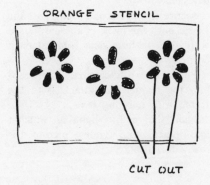

ORANGE STENCIL

CUT OUT

Make two more stencils in the same way for your other two colors.

When you have completed all three stencils, cover a large area on a table or floor with newspaper and lay the fabric on top of it.

Framed Fabric or Wallpaper Wall Hangings

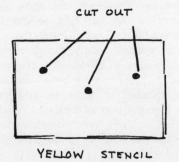

CUT OUT

YELLOW STENCIL

Be different! Everyone uses pictures and prints for wall decoration. But how many people frame and hang fabric and wallpaper? It may take a little time to get used to the idea, but these attractive and easily

made wall hangings generate a lively sense of interest, complement color schemes, and brighten dim corners. Whether you use strongly-colored prints or subdued shades, the results provide a happy harmony of color.

MATERIALS NEEDED

frame (finished or unfinished)—any size, but preferably 18×24 inches or larger
heavy cardboard—to fit the frame
fabric or wallpaper—enough to cover one side of the cardboard
white glue
scissors
masking tape
picture-hanging bracket

DIRECTIONS

If an unfinished frame is used, follow the directions outlined on pages 39–40 to finish the frame.

Cut the material or wallpaper large enough to cover one side of the cardboard, and allow for a half-inch overlap on all sides.

Cover one side of the cardboard with glue using a damp paper towel, and apply to it the fabric or wallpaper, smoothing it from the center out as you go to eliminate air bubbles and creases.

If any glue should seep through the material onto the front of the picture, wipe off the worst of it; the rest will dry clear.

Secure the overlapping edges of the fabric onto the back of the cardboard with glue, making neat folds at each corner.

Put the fabric-covered cardboard into the frame, and attach it to the frame with masking tape.

Nail the picture-hanging bracket into place, and your "picture" is ready for display.

Medieval Wall Panel

This lovely wall panel, vibrantly alive with color yet hauntingly austere, combines the smoldering brilliance of Spain and the stark simplicity of the Far East to put the touch of fire to a lackluster room.

Its special beauty tantalizes the imagination with thoughts of jewel-like mosques and shining minarets, the splendor of Saracenic grillwork, the lonely dignity of sentinel Crusader castles, and sun-drenched villas, where wisteria tumbles in a fragrant cascade.

This will be used as the background fabric squares—various colors to contrast with the background material. The number of squares required depends upon the number of openings in the panel you wish to cover
stapler
picture-hanging bracket

DIRECTIONS

Prepare the frame and wooden panel by sanding with fine and then very fine sandpaper until both are perfectly smooth. Remove all dust with a tack rag. Apply the stain of your choice with a clean rag, and wipe off any excess. Let it dry for twenty-four hours. If you prefer a darker finish, add a second coat of stain.

When the stain has dried, clean the frame and panel with a tack rag before applying a finishing coat of semigloss varnish or paste wax.

Cover one side of the cardboard with the background fabric.

MATERIALS NEEDED

1 wooden panel of a latticework-type room divider—approximately 15×-23 inches. This can be found in some lumber yards and hardware stores. These panels are normally sold in quantity for making do-it-yourself room dividers, but single panels are available for purchase
1 unfinished frame—to fit the panel
heavy cardboard—to fit the frame
wood stain—choose from any of the wood colors: walnut, maple, oak, etc.
sandpaper—fine and very fine grades
tack rag
clean rag
semi-gloss varnish or paste wax
scissors
masking tape
fabric—a solid vivid color to cover one side of the cardboard, allowing for a half-inch overlap on all sides.

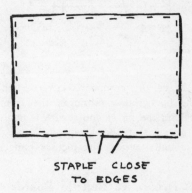

STAPLE CLOSE
TO EDGES

Staple the fabric to the edges of the cardboard. The staples should be placed as close to the edges as possible to permit their concealment by the frame. *Caution:* As you staple, pull the material taut to prevent wrinkles.

Set the panel in the frame, and turn the frame and panel face down.

Cover a number of openings in the panel to form a pattern, using fabric squares of assorted colors. Use one square of fabric for each opening to be covered. Cut each piece of material to fit the opening, so the raw edges won't show on the front of the panel. Then attach each piece of material to the back of the panel with masking tape.

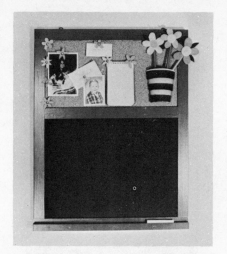

FRONT VIEW

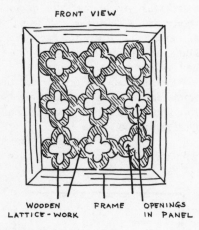

WOODEN
LATTICE-WORK
FRAME
OPENINGS
IN PANEL

Place the cardboard covered with the background fabric in the frame behind the panel and secure it to the frame with masking tape.

Finally, attach the picture hanger.

Decorative Bulletin Boards

Most of us think of bulletin boards as routine, dreary but necessary objects which normally present an atrociously unattractive and cluttered appearance. They were necessary evils in high school and college.

These much-maligned information centers can provide a surprising touch of gaiety and color to your kitchen, den, or child's room. Just try one and see if you don't agree!

MATERIALS NEEDED

bulletin board—an inexpensive one
semi-gloss enamel—any cheerful color
brush
turpentine
felt—a variety of bright colors. This comes in 10-inch squares
thumb tacks or brass upholstery tacks
pencils
1 sturdy paper cup
white glue
scissors
small notepaper tablet (optional)

DIRECTIONS

Paint the frame of the bulletin board with semi-gloss enamel. When this is dry, apply a second coat and again let it dry.

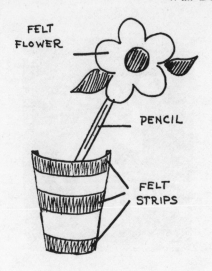

FELT FLOWER

PENCIL

FELT STRIPS

ter of each. Use these to attach a small tablet or notes to the bulletin board, or just for added interest.

Post your announcements, reminders, and chore assignments!

Easy-to-Make Prints

To give your bulletin board a look of femininity, make a flowerpot pencil holder. Cut a paper cup in half lengthwise, and use thumb tacks placed on the inside of the cup to attach it to the cork. Glue narrow strips of bright felt to the cup.

Cut large flower and leaf shapes from the felt squares and glue them to the pencil tops. Then place the pencils in the flowerpot.

Make smaller felt flowers and push a thumb tack firmly through the cen-

If you've always had a yen to cover your walls with originals, create your own pictures! This printing technique can be used to make pictures without your actually drawing them. Besides being easy to do and inexpensive, it's enormously effective. The finished products look remarkably like etch-

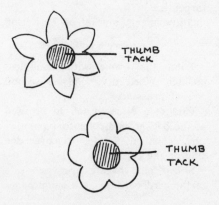

THUMB TACK

THUMB TACK

ings and engravings you've admired in stores, but felt you could not afford. Your guests will be favorably impressed with your previously undiscovered talent!

MATERIALS NEEDED

paper—heavy white writing paper or drawing paper
India ink
small paint brush
textured articles—such as leaves, coins, shells, sponges, butterflies, fabrics, screen and rope
mat board
utility knife
frame (optional)
fancy thumb tacks (optional)

DIRECTIONS

Select one or a variety of textured articles as described above. Using a brush, paint one side of each object completely with India ink. Place the paper on top of the painted article, and with your fingers rub gently over it to transfer the paint to the paper. You may have to experiment with this a bit to get the hang of it.

For a striking print, make one design combining a number of articles of varying shapes, sizes and textures.

These prints may be matted and framed, or simply matted and tacked to the wall with fancy thumb tacks. (For directions on matting or framing, see pages 39–41.)

Felt Pictures

These colorful felt pictures lighten the mood of any room and have a charm all their own. They are especially appealing in a child's room or in the kitchen, but they bring gaiety wherever they go.

MATERIALS NEEDED

frame—an inexpensive one. Any size may be used
heavy cardboard—to fit the frame
felt—a variety of colors
white glue
scissors
semi-gloss enamel—a color of your choice
paint brush
turpentine
picture-hanging bracket or brass ring

DIRECTIONS

Paint the frame with semi-gloss enamel. When dry, apply a second coat if necessary.

Choose a piece of felt to be used as the background color for your picture. Then cut the felt to cover one side of the cardboard.

Smear glue evenly over one side of the cardboard, using a damp paper towel, and attach the felt, smoothing it down carefully.

Draw a simple pattern. You may use a picture from a child's coloring book to cut apart and use as your pattern. Use your pattern to trace and cut the picture from various shades of felt. Assemble the picture on the felt background, and glue each piece into place. Insert the picture into the frame, and attach the hanging device.

Crushed Glass Wall Plaques

Take a handful of uncut emeralds, glowing with green fire; add a mass

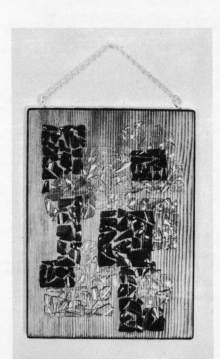

of shimmering sapphires, a sprinkling of the blazing crimson of rubies, a smattering of shining topaz, and for good measure, a generous helping of brilliantly sparkling diamonds. Toss them all together, and design a wall decoration for your home.

Sound crazy? Of course it does! But these glittering wall plaques made of crushed glass look as though you've just been gifted with the crown jewels. Their fiery radiance will illuminate the darkest corner and will provoke much excited and envious discussion.

MATERIALS NEEDED

empty glass bottles—an assortment of colors. If you can't find bottles of all the colors you wish to use, try dime store ash trays or water glasses
wooden board—15×11 inches, approximately ½ inch thick
Duco cement
sandpaper—fine and very fine grades
tack rag
wood stain or semi-gloss enamel—in a color of your choice
clean cloth—for staining only
paint brush—for painting with enamel
hammer
paper or cloth bag, or pillowcase
tweezers
empty plastic or cardboard boxes
velvet ribbon—½ inch wide, approximately 1½ yards
brass ring, picture-hanging bracket, or 2 brass rings with a brass chain

DIRECTIONS

Begin by sanding the board until it is perfectly smooth, rounding the edges slightly with sandpaper. When you have finished sanding, clean the board thoroughly with a tack rag to remove all dust and lint.

Apply your choice of stain or enamel, following the directions outlined in Chapter 3, pages 39–40.

After the stain or enamel has dried, attach your picture hanger.

To prepare the glass for use, place one bottle (or ash tray or water glass) in a paper or cloth bag or pillowcase. Hold the opening of the bag tightly closed, and hit the enclosed bottle firmly several times with a hammer. Repeat this procedure until the glass has been broken into fairly small pieces. Follow this method to crush all of the glass to be used in designing the plaque.

Suggestion: To make your work easier, keep the glass colors separated by using individual containers.

Choose bits of glass to form geometric shapes, varying the size and color of the glass chips. Use tweezers to pick up the chips in order to protect your hands from cuts and scratches.

Arrange the glass fragments on the board to create a pattern. Then, using tweezers, lift each fragment and apply Duco cement to the underside of each piece. Return each fragment to its original position on the board, pressing it down firmly. Let the glue dry for about thirty minutes.

As´a crowning touch, frame the edges of the board with narrow velvet ribbon, gluing it to the wood.

Suggestion: For that ever-fashionable black-and-white look, paint your board with black semi-gloss enamel and use crushed imitation milk glass to create a design.

Plates, Platters and Trays

You don't need a picture, a frame, a wall hanging or a plaque to dress up a wall. All you need is an unusual shape, an interesting design and a hanger.

Pick out a hand-painted tray, a trivet, a fancifully ornamented plate, a large straw mat, or your favorite ash tray; one by one, hold them up against the wall. Got the idea? A carefully balanced arrangement of two or three of these items is impressively decorative and lends a touch of the unexpected to the decor of your room.

If you don't have or can't locate an obviously eye-catching article, perhaps you'd like to try your hand at painting a tray for hanging. It's really easy to do, and you may be pleasantly surprised at your own artistic ability!

MATERIALS NEEDED

metal or wood tray

semi-gloss enamel—to be used as the background color

3 or 4 tubes of oil paint—various colors to complement the background

2 paint brushes—one very fine, and one about 1½ inches

turpentine

Treasure Gold Wax Gilt

1 adhesive picture hanger—for light trays. You may need 2 or 3 of these for a heavy tray

DIRECTIONS

Using the wide brush, paint the tray with semi-gloss enamel. When this is dry, apply a second coat of enamel and let it dry again.

With a fine paint brush, use the oil paints to decorate the tray with pleasant abstract design or boldly original flowers.

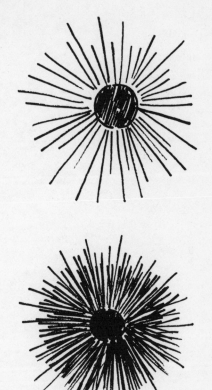

The simplest method for painting flowers is to start by drawing a small circle.

Then brush on lines radiating out from the circle. Some of the lines should be short, others slightly longer, to achieve the irregular look of petals.

Overlap the original strokes to fill out the flower, using a single color or a variety of colors.

After the oils are thoroughly dry, dab Treasure Gold onto the tray with your finger to add shining highlights.

Finally, attach the adhesive picture hanger to the back of the tray.

4. Centerpieces and Decorative Arrangements

Flower, candle and fruit arrangements add a great deal to the charm and beauty of a room and are an important part of interior decoration.

Antique Flowers

It's surprising how elegant a few plastic flowers can look if you just antique them.

Antiquing takes very little equipment and even less time. Once you've mixed the solution to dip the flowers in, keep it in a covered coffee can and you can use it over and over again. If it should start to thicken, just mix in a little more turpentine.

After you've antiqued a few flower arrangements and you get the knack of it, try antiquing tiny plastic vegetables, fruit and berries.

To the following base:

½ pint turpentine
½ small bottle of gold paint

add ½ pint of the desired varnish or stain.

Add ½ pint light oak varnish to deepen and enhance the colors and give the flowers a china or porcelain appearance.

Add ½ pint gloss or semi-gloss varnish to antique flowers of delicate colors such as white, light pink, and

yellow, or any other colors you don't want to change but do want to have a transparent, glossy look.

Add ½ pint walnut varnish for an autumn arrangement.

Add ½ pint light oak stain if you prefer an arrangement of flowers with a duller, dustier look, like that of flowers in the Flemish paintings.

DIRECTIONS

Note: Follow the same directions for each of the above formulas.

Pour the ingredients into a one- or two-pound empty coffee can and mix well.

Holding the stem, dip each flower into the solution, being sure to swish it on the bottom of the can to pick up a generous amount of gold on the petals.

Pull the flower out and shake it vigorously over the can to remove excess paint.

Hang the flowers upside down on a clothesline, using clothespins to fasten them.

Note: These can be hung to dry either outside or in, but they dry faster out of doors. However, if you hang them in the house, be sure to put plenty of newspaper on the floor to catch the drippings.

Shake the clothesline occasionally. This will prevent the accumulation of paint on the petals.

Flower and Centerpiece Arranging

At first glance, provocative floral arrangements and striking centerpieces appear intricate and prohibitively difficult to assemble. Don't be fooled —it isn't as hard as it looks!

MATERIALS NEEDED

flowers
greenery
unusual containers—baskets, bowls, pitchers, even drinking goblets
green styrofoam—to fit inside the container
wire cutters (if you're using plastic flowers)
florist clay

DIRECTIONS

(1) For your first attempt, try something very simple.

Using a tiny vase, wedge a styrofoam ball into the top opening. Vigil

candleholders make wonderful containers for miniature flower arrangements.

Cut the stems of very small antiqued flowers, leaving only about 1½ inches of stem. Push the stems firmly into the styrofoam, covering the entire ball with flowers until no styrofoam can be seen.

Add a diminutive velvet bow for an ultra-feminine touch.

(2) This radiant, springlike centerpiece is another basic type of arrangement. Put a piece of styrofoam into a basket or round bowl, and fill it completely with bright antiqued flowers.

Make the stems of the center flowers the longest, and each outward row from the center consecutively shorter, to give the arrangement a rounded look.

Attach velvet or taffeta bows on two sides of a basket or bowl.

(3) This arrangement looks particularly graceful on a small table in the living room, but it can be enlarged by adding more flowers or berries to make a sensational centerpiece for the dining-room table.

Begin by putting a very large candle in the center of a pedestaled dish, securing it with a little wax or a wad of florist clay.

Cover the entire area around the candle with flowers, miniature plastic vegetables or fruits which have been antiqued. To hold the flowers in place, first form a ring of florist clay around the bottom of the candle, and push the stems firmly into it.

For an unusual accent, paint nuts such as acorns, walnuts, or pecans

Top off the arrangement with an artificial bird or a butterfly and a velvet bow.

Use a small brass hook, which can be found in any hardware store, to suspend the basket from the ceiling.

(5) This arrangement appears elaborate, but by following these three basic steps you'll have no trouble.

Begin by putting in two tall, narrow flowers to get the desired height and width.

with varnish or gold paint and add them to your arrangement.

Make a stem for each nut by piercing a small hole in one end of it with an ice pick and inserting a short piece of wire.

Put three large flowers into the center to create a focal point.

(4) Bring a buoyant dash of color to any room with a hanging basket of antiqued flowers.

The basket can be found in either a dime store or florist shop.

Fill the bottom of the basket with flowers, and wind vines around the outside.

Then, using smaller flowers and foliage, fill out the arrangement to the desired fullness.

A cluster of grapes may also be added to one side.

ter of the bouquet and complete it with smaller flowers and foliage.

(6) The directions for this arrangement are very similar to the preceding one, but three tall flowers should be used to form the basic lines.

Calico Flowers

Add three large flowers to the cen-

These cloth flowers made of different materials are appealing wherever they are and make welcome gifts for convalescing friends or relatives.

MATERIALS NEEDED

lightweight cardboard
white glue
flexible wire
wire cutters
florist tape

In the middle of each flower make a short slit, using a razor blade. With an ice pick or scissors, poke two smaller holes on either side of the slit.

buttons (to cover)—one for each flower.

cotton material—¼ yard each of two printed and two solid colored materials

felt—10-inch squares: two different shades of green and two other colors which blend with the materials you've selected for the flowers.

flowerpot or vase

green styrofoam (to fit inside vase)

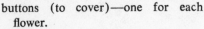

DIRECTIONS

Cut out ten or twelve 3-inch cardboard squares, depending upon the number of flowers you want to make.

Glue a 3-inch square of cotton material onto the front of the cardboard and a felt square on the back. Vary your color combinations, covering some squares with print material and others with plain. Be sure to spread the glue evenly all over the cardboard before the material is applied.

When the glue has dried, trace and cut flower shapes out of the squares.

Next, cover one button for the center of each flower with felt or cotton material, again varying the colors.

Cut a 16-inch wire stem for each flower.

Fold the wire in half and push it through the two holes on the top of the flower. (1)

TOP VIEW

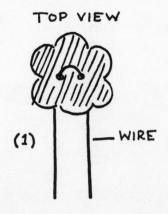

(1)   — WIRE

Insert the metal loop on the bottom of the button into the slit, so it extends through to the back of the flower. (2)

Give the back of the flowers a finished look by cutting a felt circle about the size of a fifty-cent piece. Make a small hole in the center and slip the stem through it, gluing it into place. (5)

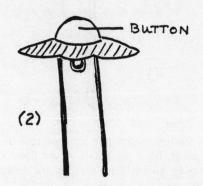

BUTTON

(2)

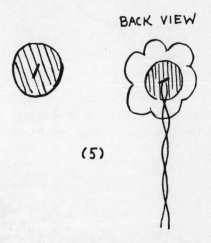

BACK VIEW

(5)

Then pull one piece of wire through the loop to hold the button securely in place, and twist the wire together, making a sturdy stem. (3–4)

Wrap green florist tape around the stem, squeezing it as you go to make it stick.

To make leaves, follow almost the same procedure as for the flowers.

Cut 1½-inch by 3-inch rectangles from the cardboard and glue material or felt on both sides. Let the glue dry, then cut out the leaves and make a small hole in the bottom of each one. (6)

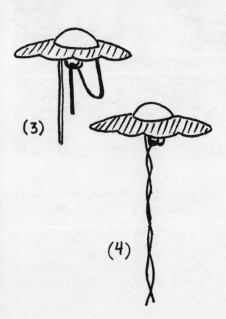

(3)

(4)

(6)

Pull a small piece of wire through the hole and twist it tightly. (7)

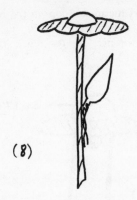

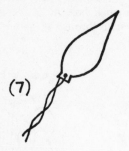

(7)

(8)

Attach it to the flower by wrapping florist tape around both the flower and leaf stems. (8)

Before putting the arrangement together, bend the petals of the flowers up to give a three-dimensional look.

Gilded or Antiqued Fruit

For sheer elegance, make a centerpiece with gilded plastic fruit. This gleaming showpiece will make you the envy of all of your friends. Don't tell them how easy it is to do!

MATERIALS NEEDED

inexpensive plastic fruit—2 apples, 2 oranges, 2 lemons, 2 bananas, a bunch of cherries, strawberries and grapes, 2 pears, 1 plum, 1 peach

and 1 pineapple will make a good arrangement
fast-drying flat black enamel spray
Treasure Gold Wax Gilt
bowl or container

DIRECTIONS

Spread newspaper under the fruit before you begin spraying to avoid getting paint on your floor or table.

Spray the fruit until it's completely covered with black paint. (Actually, you may use any color spray paint— red, dark green, or blue—but black is more effective.)

Let the paint dry thoroughly. You may find it will need a second coat if any of the original color of the fruit shows through.

When the paint is dry, get some Treasure Gold on your finger and apply it to the fruit in short strokes. The strokes should go every which way; let some of the underlying color show in various spots. It's rather like finger painting, so don't be afraid to try it!

When you've applied gold to all of the fruit, polish each piece with a soft clean rag to give it a lustrous finish.

Emphasize the fruit by using a crystal or colored glass bowl.

Sequined Fruit

This sparkling fruit arrangement glistens brightly on a candlelit table and radiates jewel-like color. It's not difficult to make, and there are very few materials needed. It's a good project to pick up and work on when you have only five or ten minutes to spare.

MATERIALS NEEDED

plastic fruit—very inexpensive fruit is easy to push pins into because it is made of a soft plastic
½-inch sequin pins
sequins—various fruit and leaf colors
small plastic boxes—keep sequins in these to separate the various colors
epoxy glue

DIRECTIONS

The procedure is very simple. Put a pin through the center of a sequin and push it into the fruit. Completely cover the fruit with bright sequins.

Various sections of the fruit can be shaded with sequins of a different color. For example, use light green on the end of a lemon, and fill in the rest with yellow, or make some of the grapes a dark purple and others a muted lavender. Add golden tones to an apple and peach and silvery highlights to strawberries.

To cover the leaves, glue green sequins in place with epoxy glue.

Pine Cone Flowers

Flowers made from pine cones have an attractive, earthy look. They

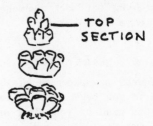

CUT PINE CONE

TOP SECTION

With heavy-duty scissors cut off the first layer of petals around the middle of the cone. (It is not necessary to do this with the top section of the pine cone.)

CUT PETALS

are especially suitable for a crisp fall or winter arrangement, but their rustic charm knows no season.

MATERIALS NEEDED

large pine cones
saw
gloss or semi-gloss spray enamel—
  two or three different colors
yellow and brown enamel
small paint brush
turpentine (to clean your brush)
wire
wire cutters
basket
styrofoam (to fit inside the basket)
velvet bow

DIRECTIONS

Saw each pine cone into two or three sections, depending upon how large it is. Approximately seven or eight cones should be sufficient to fill a basket.

Then fray the cut petals, making them look like a flower center.

Spray-paint the pine cones with the colors you have selected. When the paint has dried, cut and attach a wire stem to the bottom of each flower, and arrange them in a basket by pushing the wires into the styrofoam. (See page 57.)

FRAY PETALS

Paint the center of each flower with yellow or brown enamel, and add a large velvet bow to complete the arrangement.

Wrought-iron Sconces

If you've ever visited New Orleans and fallen in love with its wrought-iron grillwork, you're sure to find a place in your home for these delicate iron filigree sconces. Their fragile grace will call to mind the lacy balconies and antiquated charm of the Vieux Carré and will lend your home a touch of the typically romantic atmosphere to be found in New Orleans.

MATERIALS NEEDED

2 metal shelf brackets—roughly 6×6 inches
2 metal doughcut cutters
plastic flowers
flat black spray enamel
epoxy glue
4 nails or screws
2 candles

DIRECTIONS

To make one sconce, begin by gluing the handle of the doughnut cutter to the top of the metal bracket, about 2 inches from the front end of the bracket.

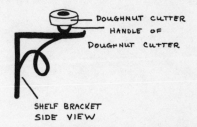

DOUGHNUT CUTTER
HANDLE OF
DOUGHNUT CUTTER

SHELF BRACKET
SIDE VIEW

The bracket must remain in an upright position overnight to allow the glue to set. This may be accomplished by propping the bracket up in an empty tin can.

Wind plastic flowers in and around the bracket, twisting the stems around the metal to hold them in place.

Now make the second sconce, following the same directions.

Then spray the sconces with flat black enamel. It may require several coats to give them the finished look of wrought iron.

Attach them to your wall by using screws or nails, and insert your selection of candles.

5. Papier-mâché Accessories

This chapter is particularly for those who are completely uninhibited. It helps if you're naturally happy-go-lucky, but if you're not, you will be by the time you've completed a few of these projects. You can work magic with papier-mâché. It can transform the most ordinary articles into bewitching objets d'art.

To make papier-mâché, all you need are newspaper and wallpaper paste. (Wallpaper paste may be bought in any hardware store.) Most papier-mâché articles are made following the same basic directions. Directions for making specific items can be found on the following pages.

BASIC DIRECTIONS

Mix water with wallpaper paste to the consistency of thick soup. Use frozen pie tins to mix the paste in; you can discard them later.

It is important to *tear* the newspaper into strips. Don't cut it. This will give the strips a feathered edge instead of a sharp one, and they will blend into one another when pasted together. To obtain a fairly straight strip, work with only one page of newspaper at a time.

Fold the newspaper in half, and tear the desired width strip by ripping down from the fold.

Be sure to cover your entire work area with plenty of newspaper. This is delightfully messy work!

NEWSPAPER

Bottles and Containers

An exotically painted papier-mâché wine bottle lends an original touch to the dinner table, or a shelf or book case.

Actually, any type of bottle covered with papier-mâché makes a picturesque container. Quart jars are perfect to cover and can be used as canisters for coffee, tea, sugar and flour. Bottles of unusual shapes make unique vases or candleholders.

(Directions for making the pencil holders shown in the photograph with the wine bottle are on pages 71–72.)

MATERIALS NEEDED

wallpaper paste
newspaper
bottle
heavy string
white glue
flat or semi-gloss enamel—one or more colors of your choice
Treasure Gold Wax Gilt (optional)
waterproof varnish
paint brush
turpentine
flat black or dark brown enamel

DIRECTIONS

There isn't much you can do to protect your hands, as this procedure is fairly messy, but you can try rubber gloves if they don't get in your way. Be sure to take off your rings because the paste is very difficult to remove when it's dry.

Prepare the paste and tear newspaper into strips approximately 1 inch thick. Divide each strip into three pieces to make it easier to handle. As you work, pull the paper strips through the paste, rubbing off any excess paste with your fingers.

Cover the entire bottle, except the top, with two layers of newspaper strips by wrapping them carefully around the bottle. Smooth each piece down with your fingers so nothing is left loose or hanging.

For small, curved areas on the bottle which are hard to cover, use very narrow, short strips. They will lie flat if they go up and down the bottle.

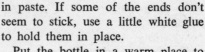

As a final coat, tear newspaper strips into squares and paste them onto the bottle, overlapping them as you work. Here again for small areas use tiny squares.

Decorate the bottle and cap with heavy string which has been soaked in paste. If some of the ends don't seem to stick, use a little white glue to hold them in place.

Put the bottle in a warm place to dry for approximately twenty-four hours. When it has dried completely, paint the bottle and cap with enamel. It may be painted one solid color or several contrasting colors. Let the enamel dry, and give it a second coat if any newspaper can still be seen.

To antique the bottle, dip a stiff brush into black or brown enamel, and wipe most of it off on newspaper until there is very little paint left on the brush. Then brush gently over the bottle, making it a little darker in some places than in others. After the antique finish has dried, give the bottle two coats of a waterproof varnish, letting it dry between coats. This makes the bottle washable.

You may rub Treasure Gold over the string designs for a more dramatic effect.

Decorative Pencil or Letter Holders and Wastebaskets

Most people throw away old tin cans because they don't know what else to do with them. With very little effort you can make a tin can, coffee can or wastebasket serviceable and remarkably lovely as well.

The size and use of the finished product may be different, but the directions for constructing them are the same.

MATERIALS NEEDED

empty can or waste basket

wallpaper paste
newspaper
heavy string or twine
beads—inexpensive necklaces
white glue
paint brush
turpentine
clear varnish
flat or semi-gloss enamel—two colors:
   one for the undercoat and one for
   antiquing
Treasure Gold Wax Gilt

DIRECTIONS

Mix the paste, and tear newspaper into strips about 1 inch wide.

Draw the strips through the paste and wrap them carefully around the can until it is completely covered with two coats of papier-mâché.

Rip newspaper strips into squares and cover the entire can with them, smoothing them out as you work.

Trim the can with calculated abandon. Wind paste-soaked string ir-

regularly around it, and scatter various-sized beads over all, using white glue to hold them firmly in place.

When the papier-mâché has dried, paint the can with two coats of enamel, letting it dry between coats.

Choose an accent color for antiquing, and dip only the very tip of a stiff brush into the paint. Wipe most

of the paint off on some newspaper, and brush gently over the surface of the can.

Let the paint dry and apply two coats of varnish.

Dab Treasure Gold onto the string, beads, and parts of the can to add a rich, metallic shine.

Ornamental Boxes

———

Old cigar boxes, empty oatmeal boxes—in fact, all empty cardboard boxes—are potentially fanciful and functional containers. Cigar boxes are especially good, because they are made of very heavy cardboard. These can be used to advantage on tables or as jewelry boxes.

Use oatmeal boxes as containers for such things as hair rollers, bath powder or yarn. Papier-mâché tissue boxes add to the decor of a bathroom, bedroom or kitchen.

You can make an ordinary recipe box attractive just by adding a little papier-mâché and paint.

Directions for making the napkin rings shown in the illustration of the boxes are to be found on page 74.

MATERIALS NEEDED

box
wallpaper paste
newspaper
white glue
felt
flat or semi-gloss enamel—at least
   two colors: one for the undercoat,
   one for antiquing, and one for decorating, if you wish
clear varnish
paint brush

turpentine
Treasure Gold Wax Gilt
Any of these can be used to add
  decorations and designs to the box:
  string, heavy cardboard, beads,
  lace, rickrack

DIRECTIONS

Select a box to be covered with
papier-mâché and follow the basic
procedure of mixing paste and tearing
newspaper strips and squares.

Apply two layers of strips and a
final layer of squares over the outside
of the box and cover.

The inside may be covered with
papier-mâché. However, it's easier to
leave it untouched, and paint it or
line it with felt when you are finished
with the outside.

When decorating the box, try several varying approaches. Play with it
a little bit until you come up with an
idea which satisfies you.

A modern design can be achieved
by arranging paste-soaked string and
beads irregularly on the box top.

Flower shapes can be formed with
string, and beads used for the center
of each flower.

Use a feminine approach to decorate a box by applying rickrack or

lace soaked in paste to the cover and sides. This will harden as it dries and looks very dainty when painted.

For a tastefully simple pattern, cut designs from heavy cardboard, glue them in place, and outline or decorate them with string.

COVER OF BOX

When your box is completed, put it away to dry. Then paint it with two coats of enamel, and antique it with another color by getting a very small amount of paint on your brush and gently brushing over the entire box. Be sure to let it dry following each layer of paint.

Next, give the box a protective coat of varnish. When this has dried, add a little spice to the box by applying Treasure Gold. Dab it on lightly with your finger so the original color shows through the gold.

To complete the box, cover the inside of it with brightly colored felt.

Napkin Rings

For a time considered outmoded and slightly passé, napkin rings have staged a triumphant comeback. Traditionally symbolic of an era of gra-

cious and graceful dining, you'll find them again proudly displayed in the most fashionable shops and department stores—in all shapes, sizes and prices!

These charming papier-mâché napkin rings, inexpensive and easy to make, will complement and enhance your prettiest linens.

MATERIALS NEEDED

cardboard tube—from the inside of a
  roll of waxed paper or foil
wallpaper paste
newspaper
heavy string
beads—from an old necklace
flat or semi-gloss enamel—a color of
  your choice
clear varnish
Treasure Gold Wax Gilt

DIRECTIONS

Using a knife with a serrated edge or a small saw, cut the cardboard tube into 1½-inch rings.

Get the paste ready, and tear newspaper into strips about 1 inch wide and 3 or 4 inches long.

Wrap the strips, which have been soaked in paste, around the cardboard ring. Cover the inside, outside and edges with approximately two layers of strips.

Decorate the napkin rings with string and beads by gluing them on in a haphazard fashion.

Set these aside until the papier-mâché is absolutely dry. Then paint them inside and out with two coats of enamel.

After this has dried, varnish the rings and let them dry again.

Rub on a little Treasure Gold. This should be applied in uneven strokes with your finger to add highlights.

Jewelry

Costume jewelry is definitely "in"! And the more capriciously designed it is, the better.

Bring your wardrobe up to date with bold, gay papier-mâché pins.

You will find them fun to make, and with a little ingenuity you can come up with a wild assortment of shapes and colors. Small, delicate pins are perfect for dressy occasions, and large, startling ones for casual wear.

Your own personal designs add individuality and glamour to the clothes you wear. These pins are not difficult to construct and are inexpensive, so why not make a batch of them?

MATERIALS NEEDED

cardboard—flexible, but not too thin. Poster board is fine
wallpaper paste
pin clasps
white paper—heavy writing paper is fine
scissors
hobby enamels—these come in a wide range of colors
white glue
glossy varnish
paint brush
turpentine
Any or all of these may be used to decorate your pins: flat buttons, string, beads

DIRECTIONS

Draw and cut the pin shapes out of cardboard; also cut the same shape from a piece of white paper.

Here are a few suggested patterns which you can enlarge and use, although you may prefer to make your own.

Mix two pans of paste. One should be fairly thin, the consistency of soup, and the other very thick, about the texture of oatmeal.

Soak the cardboard and paper shapes in the thinner paste and stick

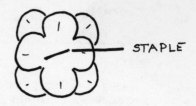

STAPLE

1 AND 2 MAKE
A FLOWER PIN
WITH DOUBLE
PETALS.

them together. The paper should be on the top of the pin to give added strength and make a smoother surface for painting.

Dab a little white glue in the center of the pin and place a button, bead, or coil of string on top of it.

Put a dab of the thicker paste on the top of each petal. It doesn't have to be smooth. When this dries it will give the petals a slight texture.

You may have to prop them up several times, since they have a tendency to droop when they dry.

Glue a pin clasp onto the back of the pin and let the glue harden before painting.

Paint the pins any color combinations you prefer with hobby enamel. It will probably take two coats, but this paint dries quickly.

To put polka dots on the petals or flower center, dip the end of a toothpick into enamel and barely touch the pin with the tip of it.

When the paint has dried, cover the pin with a coat of glossy varnish.

Earrings may be made in the same way, but on a smaller scale. Use the directions for napkin rings (section preceding Jewelry) to make matching bracelets.

To make flowers with several layers of petals, follow the same procedure, but secure the layers with a staple before applying the thick paste.

Place the pin on aluminum foil or waxed paper to dry for approximately twenty-four hours. Turn the petals up occasionally so they won't look flat.

Fruit

Colorful papier-mâché fruit can intensify interest in the kitchen or breakfast nook. Most guests just naturally drift toward the kitchen, so why not dress it up a little!

(Directions for making the newspaper flowers, shown in the photograph with papier-mâché fruit, are on pages 78–80.)

MATERIALS NEEDED

inexpensive plastic fruit
wallpaper paste
newspaper
heavy string
flat or semi-gloss enamel—a variety
  of colors to paint the fruit
black or brown enamel—for antiquing
paint brush
turpentine
clear varnish

DIRECTIONS

Stir water and wallpaper paste together. Tear newspaper into 1½-inch
squares. Paste these squares onto the
fruit until all of the plastic is completely covered. For small areas
which are hard to cover, use even
smaller squares of newspaper.

Arrange paste-soaked string on the
fruit to make interesting line designs.

Let the papier-mâché dry thoroughly and paint the fruit. Let your
imagination run wild when choosing
color schemes. Each piece may be
painted one solid color or a number
of colors.

When the enamel has dried, antique
the fruit by brushing over it very
lightly with black or brown paint.
This will accent the string designs by
adding shadows and highlights to the
fruit.

Give the fruit a finishing coat of
varnish, let it dry, and arrange in a
basket or bowl.

Newspaper Flowers

Everybody loves flowers.

You don't have to have a green thumb to create roses so realistic you can almost smell them, and whimsical, make-believe flowers. You just fold, cut and paste newspaper together.

MATERIALS NEEDED

newspaper
wallpaper paste
stapler
masking tape
scissors
flexible wire
wire cutter
florist tape
spray enamel—your choice of colors
hobby enamel (optional)—this can be
   used after the flowers have been
   sprayed with enamel, to give additional color and shading
artificial leaves
vase or bowl

DIRECTIONS

Roses

Cut a piece of newspaper into a 5×15-inch rectangle and fold it in half lengthwise. (Larger or smaller roses can be made by using more or less newspaper.)

Round both ends of the paper by cutting and roll up the strip very loosely.

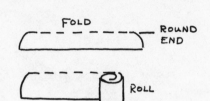

Crush the bottom of the roll tightly together and secure it with a staple.

Mix the wallpaper paste, dip your finger in it, and carefully cover the flower with paste, inside and out.

When the flower is thoroughly dampened by the paste, gently turn and form the petals. This is very easy

to do, but you may have to experiment on one or two flowers before you get the most attractive effect.

When the flowers have dried, paint them with spray enamel. Various portions of the flower, such as the center, may be painted another color by hand with hobby enamel when the spray has dried.

Make a hole in the bottom of each flower, pull a wire through the hole, and twist it together to form a stem.

Cover the hole and wire with florist tape wound tightly around it.

Add artificial leaves to the flowers by winding tape around the leaf and flower stems.

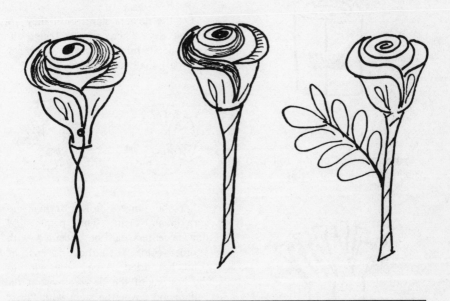

Other Flowers

Begin with a 5×15-inch newspaper rectangle and fold it in half lengthwise.

Then pleat, or gather the paper until you have made a complete circle,

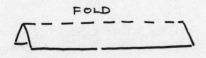

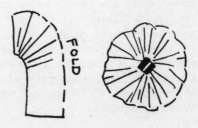

and staple it in the middle several times to hold it securely. Smear paste on both sides.

To make the center of the flower, fold a 5×8-inch piece of newspaper in half lengthwise, roll it up loosely, and tape it together.

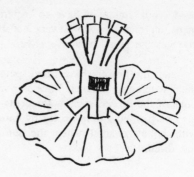

Fringe the top of the roll into approximately ¼-inch strips.

To attach this to the center of the flower, make tabs by cutting ½-inch slits around the bottom of the roll and fold them out. With your finger rub paste on all parts of the roll and place it in the center of the flower. Use tiny strips of newspaper soaked in paste to cover up the tabs and hold the pieces together.

Let the flowers stand until they are almost dry. Then cut or fringe the outer petals into any shape you wish, and curl them up a little bit.

Let the flowers finish drying and spray-paint them. The petals and flower centers can be accented with another color when the first coat of paint has dried. Attach the wire to the bottom of the flower, twist it together and cover the stem with florist tape. Finally, wrap the stems of artificial leaves and the flowers together with florist tape.

For guides on arranging the flowers see Chapter 4, page 57.

Casual Book Ends

Bookcases have a perplexing habit of shrinking visibly overnight. Nobody really understands the abrupt transi-

tion from an attractive piece of furniture to a bulging container, but all of us have been faced at one time or another with the sight of books piled on the floor, stacked on tables, thrown on chairs, jammed in closets, and ultimately stored in boxes. To help control the overflow, try these engaging book ends.

MATERIALS NEEDED

metal or wooden book ends—inexpensive ones
newspaper
wallpaper paste
heavy string
scissors
beads—optional
semi-gloss enamel—any color or a variety of colors
paint brush
turpentine
semi-gloss varnish

DIRECTIONS

Tear newspaper into approximately 1-inch squares, and mix the paste. Cover the entire vertical section of

VERTICAL SECTION OF BOOK END

each book end with three or four layers of paste-soaked squares, smoothing each square carefully as you work.

After applying the final layer of squares, decorate the book ends with heavy string which has been soaked in paste. If you choose, add a sprinkling of beads, using white glue to hold them in place.

When the papier-mâché is dry, paint the book ends with semi-gloss enamel. Let this dry, and apply a second coat.

An alternate color of semi-gloss enamel may be used on the string and bead designs to accent their importance.

The final coat of enamel must be fully dry before applying varnish.

6. Kitchen Brighteners

Bring a lively look to the kitchen by using lots of color. So much time is spent each day in the kitchen that it should be as inviting as any other room in your home.

Festive Tablecloths

A bright tablecloth makes every meal a party. It's not difficult to make, it doesn't show spots, and it launders beautifully.

Cotton material comes in such a wide variety of patterns and prints that it's fun to have several tablecloths for holiday entertaining and different seasons of the year. While you're at it, why not make a special cloth for the dining-room table, and a matching one for a card table to use when serving buffet dinners.

MATERIALS NEEDED

tape measure

cotton material
thread
fringe or braid (optional)
needle
scissors

DIRECTIONS

Measure the top of your table to determine the amount of material needed. Allow approximately 6 extra inches for a hem and overhang on each side.

Next, choose the material in a color and pattern that will add excite-

ment to the room. *Note:* As a rule, material comes in three different widths: 36 inches, 45 inches and 54 inches. Therefore, the first thing to do is to find out the width of the material you have selected. Then it will take a little arithmetic to decide on the amount needed. If the material is too narrow for your table, you might have to make a seam down the middle. Most saleswomen are happy to help you figure this out, so don't be afraid to ask.

Cut the material to the desired dimensions and sew a seam down the middle if necessary.

Make the hem about ¼ inch, turning the material under twice to conceal the raw edges. This may be sewed on the machine, or sewed by hand using small stitches.

Decorative fringe or braid may be added around the bottom of the tablecloth.

Decorative Napkins

Eliminate dull table settings with casual napkins made of bold prints, checks, and plaids.

You will find it is much less expensive to make napkins than it is to buy them. Good cotton material, particularly remnants, sells for about a dollar a yard, and many napkins can be made from one yard. Further, it is much easier to remove spots from cotton than from linen.

MATERIALS NEEDED

cotton material—a 16-inch square for
  each napkin
thread
needle
ruler
scissors

DIRECTIONS

DIRECTIONS

Cut your material into 16-inch squares. Make a ¼-inch hem, turning it under twice to hide the raw edges. Matching thread may be used to sew the hem, or for added interest, use another color: dark blue stitching on light blue napkins, or brown thread on yellow material. The hem can be sewed either by hand or by machine.

Place Mats

In Great-grandmother's day there was no such thing as "casual" entertaining. She spent hours preparing her table for guests, and by the time they finally departed she had usually reached the state of complete exhaustion.

Today most of our entertaining is deliberately casual. For spur-of-the-moment suppers, bridge parties, and luncheons, try your own personalized place mats. They save time, effort, and money!

Burlap is one of the best materials to use for making place mats. It is now made in a wide range of colors, from tangy orange to subtle green or misty blue—just about any color to suit your fancy. Burlap is fairly stiff, so the place mats will hold their shape, and it's very easy to handle, even for beginners. In fact, you should be able to make at least eight of these in an hour.

MATERIALS NEEDED

colored burlap—you will be able to get about six place mats from one yard of material.

scissors
thread—the same color as the burlap
needle
yardstick

DIRECTIONS

Cut the burlap into 12×18-inch rectangles. Follow one thread across the material when you cut, to get it perfectly straight.

Turn under a very tiny hem on two sides of the place mat, and stitch by hand or machine.

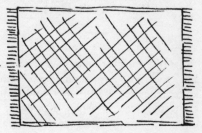

FRINGE ON SIDES

To finish it, make a 1-inch fringe on the other two sides by pulling off the threads of material.

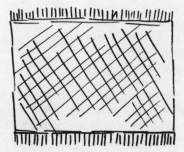

FRINGE ON TOP AND BOTTOM

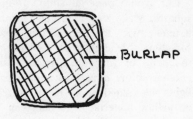

FRONT

BURLAP

Cover the edges with ribbon by overlapping it onto the front and back of the potholder and sew it securely in place, either by hand or by machine.

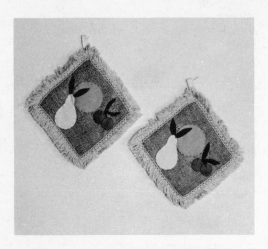

Fancy Potholders

Take a look around your kitchen. Do you see any potholders? You know they're useful, but did you know they can also give a designer's touch to the decor of your kitchen?

MATERIALS NEEDED

inexpensive potholders
colored burlap—buy enough to cover one side of the potholders
thread
grosgrain ribbon—2 inches wide and 2 yards long. This should match the color of the burlap
2 yards of fringe
scissors
needle
felt (various colors)—usually comes in 8×10-inch squares
straight pins

DIRECTIONS

The burlap should be cut the same size as the potholder. Then lay it on the front side of the potholder and pin it in place.

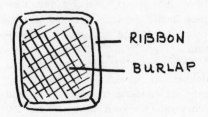

FRONT

RIBBON

BURLAP

Attach and sew the fringe to the front of the potholder, being sure to cover the ribbon.

FRONT

Draw and cut fruit or vegetable shapes from brightly colored felt and arrange them on the burlap. If you have trouble drawing a pattern, cut pictures from a magazine and trace around them.

Sew around the edges of each object, using very small stitches.

Finally, make a loop out of ribbon and sew it to one of the corners so the potholder can be hung on the wall.

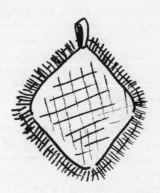

Colorful Canisters

The delightful charm of these canisters belies their functional purpose. Their humble origin (the dime store) artfully concealed, they'll give your kitchen an enviable, well-dressed look.

MATERIALS NEEDED

1 set of metal canisters—inexpensive ones
semi-gloss enamel—white for the base coat, a bright color to be used for antiquing, and 2 or 3 accent colors for decorative purposes
2 paint brushes—one fine, and one 1½ inches
turpentine
steel wool—triple 0 grade. (This is needed only if the canisters have a very shiny finish)
1 small sponge
scissors
lightweight cardboard
semi-gloss varnish

DIRECTIONS

If the canisters have a shiny finish,

it is necessary to rub them vigorously with steel wool so paint will adhere to the surface.

Before painting, wash the canisters with soap and water, and dry them thoroughly.

Then paint the canisters with the white base coat. Let it dry, and apply another coat of white enamel. Let this dry for at least 24 hours.

To antique the canisters, dip a stiff brush into the enamel you have chosen for antiquing. Wipe the brush on newspaper to remove most of the paint, and lightly brush the remainder onto the base coat, using uneven strokes. Be sure to let some of the base coat show through the antique finish.

Before proceeding, allow the canisters to dry completely.

Designs may be added to the canisters by using stencils. You may find this easier than freehand drawing.

To make stencils, first cut two 4-inch squares of lightweight cardboard.

In the center of one square, draw a simple flower shape, approximately 1 inch in diameter.

DRAW FLOWER SHAPE

Cut around the outline of the flower, until the flower shape can be removed from the cardboard and dis-

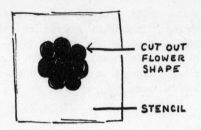

CUT OUT FLOWER SHAPE

STENCIL

carded. Now you are left with a cardboard square with a hole in the middle. This is one of your stencils.

In the center of the second cardboard square draw a similar flower shape, approximately 2 inches in diameter.

Follow the same procedure as before, cutting out and discarding the flower shape, retaining the stencil.

Using scissors, cut two 1-inch chunks from a small sponge.

With one hand hold a stencil firmly on the canister; with the other, dip the end of a sponge chunk into one of your accent colors.

Touch the paint-soaked sponge to newspaper to remove any large accumulations of paint. Now dab the sponge over the opening in the stencil several times. When the paint forms the flower shape, remove the stencil.

Make a number of flowers around the canister using this same stencil. Then switch to the other stencil and repeat the procedure, using a different accent color and a clean piece of sponge.

When the canisters are dry, outline the flower shapes with a third accent color, using a fine brush.

After this has dried, add a protective coat of semi-gloss varnish.

Salt and Pepper Shakers

Salt and pepper shakers contribute much to the mood and flavor of a meal, as well as to the decor of your table. So, for a change of pace, instead of being traditional (silver and crystal) or contemporary (wood and pottery), be a real swinger and match your canisters with these sassy salt and pepper shakers.

MATERIALS NEEDED

metal salt and pepper shakers
semi-gloss enamel—white for the base coat, a perky color to be used for antiquing, and 2 or 3 accent colors for decorative purposes
2 paint brushes—one fine and one 1½ inches
turpentine
steel wool—triple 0 grade. (This is needed only if the salt and pepper shakers have a very shiny finish)
1 small sponge
scissors
lightweight cardboard
semi-gloss varnish

DIRECTIONS

Follow the same directions as outlined in the previous section.

The most important thing to remember when making these is that the holes in the top of each shaker must be kept open. To accomplish this, after each coat of paint has been applied, clean the holes by carefully inserting and removing a toothpick.

You can make your own salt and pepper shakers by using empty medicine bottles which have a plastic cap:

First, wash the bottles thoroughly. Then heat the point of an ice pick, and pierce small holes in the plastic covers. These may be painted, antiqued or covered with papier-mâché. Properly disguised, they add a piquant touch to your table.

Since they're so easy to make, why not have several sets for special occasions?

Wooden Catch-all

The days of dingy kitchen utensils are gone forever. In the past few

Begin by thoroughly cleaning the rack with a tack rag to remove all lint and dust. This will insure a smoother finish.

Then paint the rack with semi-gloss enamel and let it dry. If necessary, apply a second coat of enamel. When the paint is dry, attach the rack to the wall, using two nails or screws.

Now ransack your kitchen for interesting utensils, basing your selection on color and shape, and hang them on the rack in an appealing arrangement.

Pictures for Your Kitchen

years, all kitchen tools have undergone a thorough glamorizing process. Manufacturers are now producing pots and pans in such warmly glowing colors that it seems a shame to hide them in a cupboard.

If you've a number of kitchen articles you'd like to show off, use this catch-all to display them, and give your kitchen a new vitality.

MATERIALS NEEDED

expandable wooden hat rack
2 nails or 2 screws
hammer
semi-gloss enamel—a good accent
  color for your kitchen
paint brush
turpentine
tack rag
an assortment of kitchen utensils—
  coffee mugs, colorful pots and pans,
  potholders, wooden or enamel serving spoons and forks, or any decorative kitchen object which may
  be hung on small wooden pegs

Kitchen walls are too often like Cinderella; the stepchild of the home, sadly neglected, drab. And like Cinderella, they are potentially beautiful, charming and worthy of attention.

Since you have to live with your kitchen walls, why not adopt the role of fairy godmother, and make them attractive? You'll find your efforts well worthwhile, especially since your brand of magic won't vanish at the first stroke of midnight!

A kitchen is necessarily utilitarian, but it needn't have a merely useful appearance. You can give it a breezy look of leisurely living with imaginative wall decorations.

A planned but casual arrangement of decoupaged recipes, chopping boards, ornamental potholders, whimsically painted pottery plates or framed embroidery samplers can give a formerly barren wall a fresh, new look.

If your taste runs to water colors, oils and engravings, try an assortment of these. You'll be surprised to see how well they, too, fit into the pattern of your kitchen.

There's really no limit to the kind of wall decoration you may use in a kitchen. Just let your good taste be your guide. All it takes is some imagination and an eye for color.

7. Fabric-covered Accessories

FABRIC-COVERED ACCESSORIES

Revel in color!

Brilliant crimson, strawberry pink, buttercup yellow, mint-julep green, pungent tangerine, Mediterranean blue, pecan brown—give ordinary household objects an appearance which will attract the attention of even the most oblivious male. Imagination, glue, fabric and trim are the most important ingredients needed to make these original creations.

heavy cardboard accordion-type file
white glue
scissors
½ yard heavy cotton material—any color and pattern
gummed labels—look for these in a dime store.
colored braid trim (optional)

DIRECTIONS

Measure the front panel of the file

Handy File

Do you have trouble keeping receipts, bills, letters or recipes? A fabric-covered file can be the perfect answer to your problem. It's an easy and attractive way to organize papers so they can be found quickly when you need them.

A file also makes an ideal gift for the student who has to keep track of class notes and term papers.

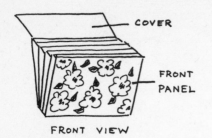

COVER

FRONT
PANEL

FRONT VIEW

The outside panels and cover may be decorated further with ornamental braid. When the glue has dried thoroughly, the file is ready for use.

Wastebaskets

and cut the material to fit, adding ¼ inch on all sides.

Cover the entire front of the file with glue, spreading it evenly with a damp paper towel.

As you apply the material, turn under a ¼-inch hem on all four sides. Smooth the material carefully, from the center out, to remove any folds or air bubbles.

Measure and cut one piece of material to fit the back panel and cover. Again allow ¼ inch for a hem on each side, and glue the material into place.

Put a champagne label on your wastebaskets and take them out of the corners!

Select your fabrics to make them sophisticated, extravagantly colorful, or quietly beautiful.

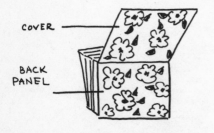

COVER

BACK
PANEL

The inside of the file has approximately twenty sections. Place a gummed label, with the title of each topic neatly printed on it, on the top of each divider.

MATERIALS NEEDED

metal wastebasket—any size and shape

½ yard material—heavy cotton. For a very large basket you might need a full yard of material

white glue

scissors

tape measure

braid or velvet ribbon 1 inch wide— to match or contrast with the material

DIRECTIONS

Measure the wastebasket and add an extra ½ inch to the top, bottom and side seam measurements. Cut the material to your specifications.

Cover the outside of the wastebasket with glue. To keep your fingers from getting sticky, spread the glue with a damp paper towel.

Then place the material on the wastebasket and turn under a half inch on the top, bottom and sides to cover the raw edges. Don't be concerned about glue that may seep through the material. Wipe off any excess, and the rest will dry clear.

For your first attempt, you might want to do a wastebasket with straight up and down sides, although baskets

Pencil and Letter Holders

Are pencils at a premium in your home? Can you never find one when you need it? If so, these easy-to-make pencil holders were designed with you in mind.

For those old letters you can't bear to throw away, make a matching letter holder.

SMALL
TUCK

with slanted sides aren't much harder to do. Simply take several small tucks around the bottom as you glue the material down.

When you have successfully covered the basket, trim the top and bottom with braid or velvet ribbon by gluing it carefully in place. If the braid doesn't stick at first, put in a few straight pins to hold it securely, and remove them when the glue has dried.

MATERIALS NEEDED

small tin can—to make a pencil holder.

letter holder—inexpensive, cardboard ones

¼ yard heavy cotton material— choose a gay print

scissors

white glue

tape measure

braid or narrow velvet ribbon—to harmonize with the material

felt

DIRECTIONS

Measure your can or letter holder and allow for an extra ½ inch on all sides. Then cut the material accordingly.

Cover the can with glue, spreading it with paper towels, and apply the material. Turn under ½ inch of the material on the top, bottom and side seam to finish off the edges.

Decorate the holder with braid or velvet ribbon by gluing it to the material.

Finally, line the inside of your pencil or letter holder with brightly colored felt.

Lamp Shades

Don't throw away old lamp shades! You can quickly revive and salvage them and save yourself a lot of money. By covering the shade with lush floral prints, vital solid colors, or subtle hues, it will look like new and give a lift to the whole room.

For a high-fashion look, cover inexpensive lamp shades to match your curtains, or try covering a bedside lamp and several matching throw pillows for the bed.

MATERIALS NEEDED

lamp shade
white glue
scissors
heavy material—enough to cover the shade
braid, velvet ribbon, or grosgrain ribbon—to match the material

DIRECTIONS

Measure the lamp shade and cut the material ½ inch larger than your measurements.

Spread glue lightly over the lamp shade, being sure to cover the entire surface. Use damp paper towels to apply the glue.

Then cover the shade with your material, and turn under the raw edges as you work.

For lamp shades with slanted sides, take tiny tucks around the top to take in the extra material. The tucks should all be the same size, and evenly

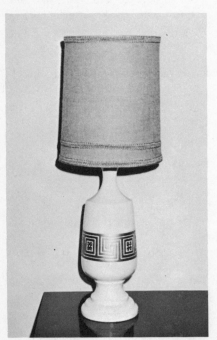

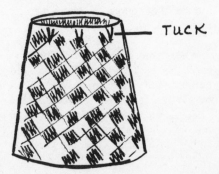

TUCK

spaced. The tucks won't show, because they will be covered with braid or ribbon.

Trim the top and bottom of the lamp shade with the braid or ribbon by gluing it to the material. Use straight pins to hold it until the glue dries, and then remove the pins.

Napkin Rings

For frivolous occasions, try these unusual fabric-covered napkin rings to spark your table setting with a riot of color.

MATERIALS NEEDED

cardboard tube—from the middle of a waxed-paper roll
knife—with a serrated edge
white glue
scissors
ruler
velvet or grosgrain ribbon, or material—the ribbon should be 1½ inches wide and approximately 7 inches long for each napkin ring. You will need ¼ yard of material

DIRECTIONS

Measure and cut the cardboard tube into 1¼-inch rings. This can be cut easily by using a knife with a serrated edge. If the sides of the rings become a little jagged, trim them with scissors.

Ribbon-covered Napkin Rings

Choose velvet or grosgrain ribbon in a variety of bright colors and cut into 7-inch pieces. Rub glue onto the cardboard ring and cover it with ribbon.

Material-covered Napkin Rings

Cut the fabric into 2×7-inch strips. Glue this over the cardboard ring, turning under the extra material to finish the edges. Optional: Add gold braid or lace.

Useful Boxes

You're familiar with that small, frugal voice that whispers, "Save it!" You probably have cupboards, draw-

ers and closets full of things you're saving, and among the contents you are likely to find empty boxes of all shapes and sizes.

Half the fun of a project like this is the idea that you're getting something for nothing.

Here are basic directions for covering three different types of boxes, although any box can be covered in a similar manner.

MATERIALS NEEDED

box
fabric—enough to cover the box
white glue
tape measure
braid, rickrack or lace—to go with
the material
scissors

DIRECTIONS

Tissue Box

Cut one piece of material large enough to cover the top of the box and allow for a 1-inch overlap on the sides.

Spread glue on the box top and attach the material. Stretch the material slightly as you put it in place so it will be nice and smooth. Then glue the overlapping material down, snipping the corners of the material to make a neat fold.

Find the original hole on the top of the box under the material and make a slit in the material from one end of the hole to the other.

Cut a second piece of material long enough to cover all four sides of the box, and wide enough to allow for a hem on the top and bottom.

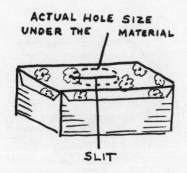

As if you were cutting a pie, make about eight cuts from the center of the material to the edge of the hole.

Glue the material to the box, turning under the raw edges on the top, bottom and side seam.

Add a little vitality to the box by trimming it with ornamental braid.

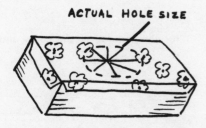

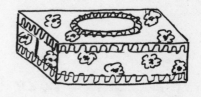

Oatmeal Box

Turn and glue these flaps to the underside of the box top.

Measure the box to determine the amount of material needed and cut it

1 inch longer and wider than the actual size of the box.

Rub glue all over the outside of the box and place the material on it smoothly. Turn under ½ inch of material around the bottom and at the side seam. On the top, fold the extra ½ inch inside the box and glue it in place.

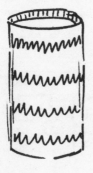

Cut a round piece of material 3 inches bigger in diameter than the box cover.

Glue this circle to the cover, and take small tucks around the sides to make the material conform to the round shape.

Turn and glue the ends of the material to the inside of the cover.

The inside of the box and cover may be lined with felt to give it a finished look. Decorate the outside with bright braid, rickrack, or lace.

Cigar Box

Cut one long piece of material to cover the four sides of the box. Be sure to leave a little extra material to turn under on the top, bottom and side seam.

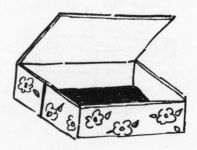

Cover the box with glue and apply the material, turning under the edges as you smooth it down.

Measure the cover and add 1 inch to each side when you cut the material.

Glue the material to the cover and

turn under a 1-inch hem along the back. The material on the cover should start where the material on the back of the box leaves off.

Turn and glue 1 in to the inside of the cove three sides. Snip the cc material so it will fold u

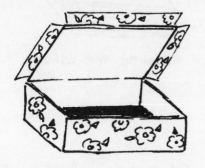

Line the inside of the box with felt and embellish the outside with various trimmings.

Unique Book Covers

Telephone directories are essential, but they certainly don't add to the decor of a room. Why not do something about it? Conceal unattractive exteriors with an explosion of color!

Other books, such as address books, photo albums and cook books can be dramatized in the same way.

Telephone Book Cover

MATERIALS NEEDED

½ yard fabric—heavy cotton or burlap in a color of your choice
ruler
white glue
scissors
stapler
heavy cardboard—tag board will
  work
decorative braid

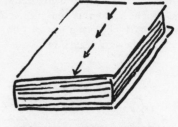

MEASURE THE LENGTH
OF COVER

DIRECTIONS

Measure the total width of the
phone book cover and add 10 inches
to your figures.

Cut one piece of cardboard to these
specifications. Fold the cardboard to

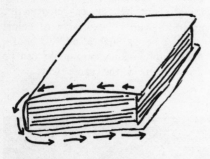

MEASURE TOTAL WIDTH
OF COVER

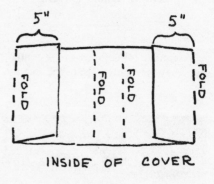

INSIDE OF COVER

fit around the phone book and turn in
5 inches on both sides.

Measure the length of the cover,
adding an extra inch to the measurements.

Staple these 5-inch flaps to the edge
of the cardboard.

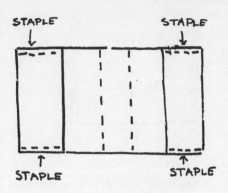

STAPLE   **STAPLE**

STAPLE   **STAPLE**

INSIDE OF COVER

Glue a piece of fabric onto the outside of the cover and overlap it ½ inch on the inside.

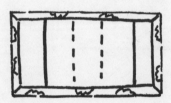

INSIDE OF COVER

Complete the camouflage with braid.

Permanent Book Covers

Some book covers do not need to be removable and can be attached directly to the original cover.

MATERIALS NEEDED

fabric—enough to cover the book.

Use a heavy material such as cotton or burlap
ruler
white glue
scissors
braid

DIRECTIONS

Cut the material large enough to cover the book and overlap 1 inch on the inside.

Spread glue evenly over the book cover and carefully attach the material.

Turn and glue 1 inch of material to the inside cover, making neat folds at the corners.

Carry through the disguise with braid.

Shower Curtain

Make your bathroom strikingly different with a colorful shower curtain.

It's advisable to check to see if the material is preshrunk, or you may end up with a mini-curtain.

Protect the curtain from water by using a plastic liner.

While you're at it, you can also make matching window curtains.

MATERIALS NEEDED

4½ yards of fabric—36 inches wide.
  Heavy cotton is best, and can be
  laundered easily
ball fringe (optional)
thread
sewing machine

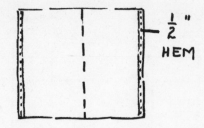

Then fold and sew a 4-inch hem on the top and bottom of the curtain.

shower curtain hooks or hangers
yardstick
scissors
plastic shower curtain liner

DIRECTIONS

Cut the material in half so the 2 panels are each 2¼ yards long, and sew them together.

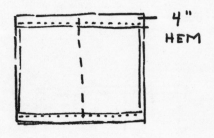

Evenly space 12 buttonholes across the top of the curtain for the hooks.

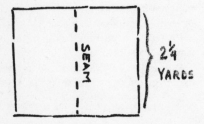

Make a ½-inch hem on both sides, turning the material under twice to conceal the raw edges.

Suggestion: Ball fringe may be added to the bottom of the curtain.

Throw Pillows

A recent survey of neighbors, friends and relatives indicated that no one really knows what to do with old bed pillows. If your supply of old bed pillows has reached alarming proportions, here is a way to cut them down to size. They can be remade into fashionable throw pillows to accentuate a davenport or bed.

MATERIALS NEEDED

old pillow
scissors
thread
needle
fabric—enough to cover the pillow;
    about 1 yard of material
rickrack or braid (optional)

DIRECTIONS

If you are using Dacron or foam-rubber pillows simply cut the pillow in half to make two small pillows. For very small ones, cut into fourths.

Divide the stuffing evenly between the pillows, and sew the open ends of each pillow closed.

To cut feather pillows in half sew two rows of stitches, about an inch apart, through the middle of the pillow and then cut the pillow between the rows of stitching. This will keep the contents intact.

Cut one piece of material large enough to cover the front and back

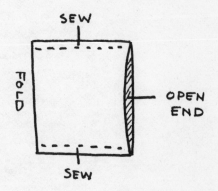

of the pillow. Fold the material in half and sew two of the sides together, leaving the fourth side open.

Turn the cover so the seams are on the inside, and slip the pillow in through the opening.

Sew the opening together by hand using tiny stitches. These stitches can be easily removed when you want to launder the cover.

Rickrack or braid may be sewed to the cover.

Footstools

Give your spirits as well as your feet a lift with these pretty and practical footstools. Cover them with lively prints, checks or plaids, sober or vivid solid hues, and see what a complementary addition they are to any room. Just looking at them soothes tired feet!

MATERIALS NEEDED

1 small footstool with detachable round cushion

heavy cotton fabric—enough to cover the top and sides of the cushion, and to allow for a 2-inch overlap on the bottom

thread—1 spool to match the fabric, and 1 spool of heavy-duty (extra-strong) thread

needle

scissors

straight pins

DIRECTIONS

Remove the cushion from the footstool frame and cut a circle of fabric large enough to cover the top, the sides, and allow for a 2-inch overlap on the bottom of the cushion.

Place the fabric circle on a table with the right side (finished side) face down.

Next, turn the cushion upside down, and put it on top of the fabric, centering it.

BOTTOM OF
CUSHION

Pull the fabric up over the sides of the cushion, and overlap it onto the bottom.

Push straight pins through the fabric into the cushion to hold it together temporarily.

Take small, even tucks around the sides of the cushion to make the fabric conform to the round shape. Use a straight pin to hold each tuck in place until you have completed all of them.

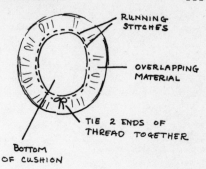

RUNNING STITCHES

OVERLAPPING MATERIAL

TIE 2 ENDS OF THREAD TOGETHER

BOTTOM OF CUSHION

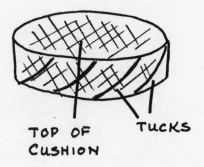

TOP OF CUSHION   TUCKS

Using small stitches, sew each tuck with matching thread, and remove the straight pins.

To hold the covering material taut and wrinkle-free, use heavy-duty thread to sew the overlapping edges on the bottom of the cushion.

This may be done by using a running stitch, and tying the two ends of the thread tightly together.

Or take large stitches across and up and down the bottom of the cushion, pulling the overlapping edges of the fabric toward the center.

Remove all straight pins and replace the cushion in the frame of the footstool.

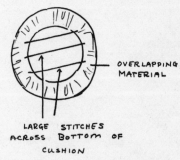

OVERLAPPING MATERIAL

LARGE STITCHES ACROSS BOTTOM OF CUSHION

BOTTOM VIEW OF CUSHION

8. Finishing and Refinishing Furniture

You may not think of yourself as a carpenter, but you never know what you can do with an old piece of furniture until you try.

Working on furniture for your home is tremendously rewarding, not only because of the satisfied glow you feel when you've finished your masterpiece, but also because it keeps the lid on your budget.

Unfinished Furniture

The simplest way to try working with furniture is to begin with a piece of unfinished furniture. This furniture is generally made of pine, and is relatively inexpensive. It can be bought or ordered in most department stores, discount stores, and some hardware stores.

Prepare the surface for painting by sanding it with fine and very fine sandpaper until it is perfectly smooth. (Remember, the smoother the sanding, the more professional the finished piece.)

When you are through, remove all the dust by rubbing over the wood with a tack rag. (Buy this in a paint or hardware store.) Any dust that remains will show up on the finished surface and will mar the appearance of your furniture.

For suggestions and directions on completing your furniture, see the Painting, Antiquing and Staining section of this chapter.

Old Furniture

Half the excitement of working with old "junk" furniture is hunting for it and visualizing what it will look like once you've given it a new lease on life. Local junk shops, Salvation

115

Army stores and Goodwill stores are excellent places to search for something to work on. Try to choose furniture which is in fairly good condition, and your work will be much easier.

For experimental purposes select a small, simple piece of furniture.

Prepare Furniture for Antiquing

If you decide to antique the furniture, it is not necessary to remove the old finish unless it is in very poor condition.

Thoroughly clean the entire surface of the furniture, first with a rag dampened with ammonia, and then with vinegar to take off old wax, grit and grime.

Fill any large nicks, scratches, dents, or holes with plastic wood filler, following the manufacturer's directions. (Buy plastic wood in a hardware store.) Be sure to fill the holes slightly higher than the furniture's surface so they can be sanded down even with the wood and will not show. Let the filler dry for twenty-four hours before sanding.

Sand the furniture, starting with medium-grade sandpaper, and then following up with fine sandpaper, until it is very smooth. This is the most important step in achieving a truly fine finish.

For sanding large areas, wrap the

sandpaper around a small block of wood. This makes it easier to handle, and helps you apply more pressure without tiring your fingers. *Important!* Always sand in the same direction as the grain of the wood.

When you have finished sanding, remove all dust with a clean cloth and then with a tack rag. Remember, any dust you leave will show when you paint, so don't do a slipshod job.

Your furniture is now ready for antiquing. You will find directions for this procedure in the Painting, Antiquing and Staining section of this chapter.

Prepare Furniture by Removing Old Finish

Sometimes the old finish can be taken off simply by sanding the furniture, but generally it's necessary to use a paint and varnish remover. (Ask the salesman in your hardware store to recommend a good remover.) Brush on the remover with an old paint brush, and wait until the finish becomes soft. Don't work on too large an area at one time. (Try about 1 square foot.)

Then, using a putty knife, scrape off the softened paint. For stubborn areas, try fine steel wool or a toothbrush to remove the paint.

It may be necessary to apply a second coat of remover if any paint still remains.

Clean the paint remover off following the manufacturer's directions, and let the furniture dry thoroughly.

At this point, follow the directions found in the first paragraph under *Prepare Furniture for Antiquing* to fill gouges, and sand.

Painting, Antiquing and Staining

Once you have prepared your furniture the hardest part of refinishing lies behind you. Now you are ready to select and put on a new finish. There are many possibilities, so you must consider each, and how it will blend with the room decor you already have.

If you have found a beautiful piece of wood under the old paint you may not want to do anything but give it a coat or two of a good satin finish varnish, followed by several coats of paste wax.

The point to remember when selecting your supplies is that the final outcome can be only as good as the quality of the materials you choose.

Painting

In some instances you might wish to paint the furniture a solid color to harmonize with the color scheme of your room.

MATERIALS NEEDED

flat or semi-gloss enamel—any color
semi-gloss varnish
paint brush
turpentine
steel wool—triple 0 grade
tack rag

DIRECTIONS

First, be sure the piece of furniture is completely free of dust.

Then apply one coat of enamel, brushing with long smooth strokes in the same direction as the grain of the wood, and let it dry.

Before putting on a second coat of enamel, wipe over the furniture with a tack rag to remove any dust particles. This must be done each time you put on another layer of paint or varnish.

When the enamel has dried, apply a coat of varnish and let it dry.

Rub steel wool over the entire surface very lightly to remove any bubbles or lumps which may have appeared, and give it a final coat of varnish.

This should be followed with another light application of steel wool, and a coat of paste wax.

Antiquing

In the last few years this has become a very popular way to refinish furniture. It's especially appealing because it is not necessary to remove the finish from old furniture before antiquing it. The process can also be applied to new, unpainted furniture.

If you are not familiar with antiqued furniture, the idea is to give it a mellowed, aged look. This effect is achieved by first painting the furniture with a solid enamel base coat of any color, and then applying a thin glaze of another color on top of the base coat. The glaze is put on to add shadows, highlights and shading, but the base coat can still be seen through it.

It's possible to buy complete antiquing kits to do your furniture, but it's more fun and more creative to make your own. Besides, it's less expensive!

MATERIALS NEEDED

flat or semi-gloss enamel—any color. This is used as a base coat
1 tube of artist oil paints—in a color to contrast with the base coat. This is used to make the glaze
turpentine
paint brush
clean rag
cheesecloth or terry-cloth rag
mixing pan—use a frozen pie tin

DIRECTIONS

Here are a few suggested color combinations to use, but there is an infinite number of possible combinations.

White enamel base coat with *Raw* or *Burnt Umber (Dark Brown), Yellow Ochre (Mustard Gold), Chromium Oxide Green (Olive Green), Blue,* or *Red oil paint glaze.*

Red enamel base coat with *White, Black, Raw* or *Burnt Umber oil paint glaze.*

Beige or Cream enamel base coat with *Raw or Burnt Umber, Yellow Ochre, Black, Chromium Oxide Green, Red oil paint glaze.*

Green enamel base coat with *White, Black, Darker Green, Raw* or *Burnt Umber oil paint glaze.*

Blue enamel base coat with *White, Black, Darker Blue,* or *Raw* or *Burnt Umber oil paint glaze.*

Yellow enamel base coat with *Orange, Raw* or *Burnt Umber,* or *Chromium Oxide Green oil paint glaze.*

Brown enamel base coat with *Black,* or *Chromium Oxide Green oil paint glaze.*

After you have selected your supplies you are ready to begin antiquing.

Rub the furniture with a tack rag to be sure all dust has been removed. Then paint it with two layers of the base coat, letting it dry thoroughly between layers.

When the second coat of enamel has dried completely, apply the glaze.

Mix the oil paint with enough terpentine to make the glaze about the same consistency as the enamel you have just used as your base coat.

Dip a clean rag into the glaze, and wipe it onto the furniture, covering the base coat. Let this set for about five minutes until it becomes tacky (sticky), but not dry. Using a clean textured rag, such as terry cloth or cheesecloth, begin wiping off the glaze so a thin layer of glaze remains over the base coat. The textured cloth will give the glaze a slightly streaked, uneven appearance, which is the effect you are trying to achieve. Leave the glaze a little heavier around the edges, corners and moldings.

Be sure to work on only a small area at a time so the glaze remains workable. If it should become too dry, dampen your rag lightly with turpentine.

Let the glaze dry twenty-four hours or more, and then give the furniture two coats of protective varnish.

An unusual treatment of antiqued furniture is to give it a spattered or wormhole effect. This should be done after the glaze has dried and before the varnish is applied.

To do this use black or brown enamel. Dip a small, stiff brush, such as a toothbrush, into the enamel. Stand back from the furniture several feet, and then flick the paint on it in tiny droplets.

It's a good idea to do this outside, or your walls may also acquire a wormhole look!

Staining

If you prefer a natural wood look, and your furniture is in good condition, then staining may be your choice of finish.

MATERIALS NEEDED

stain—in any of the wood colors: walnut, maple, oak, etc.
paint brush
clean rags
turpentine
semi-gloss varnish
paste wax
steel wool—triple 0 grade
tack rag

DIRECTIONS

Apply the stain to a clean, dust-free surface by wiping it on with a rag. Use another cloth to wipe off any excess stain that does not soak into the wood.

When the stain has dried, lightly rub steel wool over the furniture and apply a second coat of stain. Again, when it is dry, go over it with steel wool. Then varnish it, let it dry, and again rub lightly with steel wool.

Follow the same procedure and varnish once more.

Finish with a coat of paste wax.

A colored stain, such as red, green, or blue, can be easily made and applied in the same manner. To make a colored stain, thin an enamel of any color with an equal amount of turpentine, and use it the same as you would a regular wood stain.

9. Unusual Conversation Pieces

Are you looking for something really extraordinary? This chapter is a treasure-trove of such items. Some of them are very easily constructed, but others will be a real test of your skills.

Antique Ash Trays

If you like the look of those expensively magnificent hand-blown crystal or mosaic ash trays but haven't felt your budget could stand the strain, these are for you. Scatter them generously around your home; maybe those people who persist in using your best china saucers for ash trays or those who carelessly leave a trail of ashes behind them will take the hint.

These are deceiving. They look so luxurious that no one would guess they started out as mere dime store ash trays.

MATERIALS NEEDED

clear glass ash tray—any size
small picture—to fit the bottom of the ash tray
white glue
plastic spray
flat black enamel
water-resistant flat varnish
Treasure Gold Wax Gilt
paint brush
turpentine
paper towels

DIRECTIONS

Cut a small picture from a magazine, greeting card, or gift-wrap paper to fit the bottom of the ash tray.

If there is any writing or print on the back of the picture, paint it with flat black enamel and let it dry. This will keep the lettering from showing through.

Spray both sides of the picture twice with plastic, letting it dry between coats.

Spread white glue evenly over the picture and place the picture on the

123

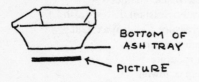

BOTTOM OF
ASH TRAY

PICTURE

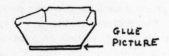

GLUE
PICTURE

bottom of the ash tray so it is visible from the right side of the dish.

Vigorously rub over the picture with a damp paper towel or a small wooden roller to be sure it is com-

pletely affixed to the glass. The glue becomes transparent and will not detract from the picture.

When the glue has dried thoroughly, apply Treasure Gold to the outer sides of the ash tray. This should be put on with your finger in short, blotchy strokes similar to finger painting. Be sure to leave small areas which are not covered by the gold. When you are through, let it set for twenty-four hours before continuing.

Next, carefully paint the outer sides and bottom of the ash tray with flat black enamel. Do not rebrush any area, or the gold may smear.

When the enamel is dry, apply a second coat and dry again.

Complete the job by giving the sides and bottom five coats of waterproof varnish, letting it dry twenty-four hours between each layer.

Handsome Wooden Boxes

―――――――

These distinctive wooden boxes, when prominently displayed on a coffee table, desk or dresser, provide that extra flourish which makes any room something special. Finished boxes such as these are quite expensive to buy, but you can make them for a comparatively low cost.

If you work carefully and meticulously, the box will acquire a rich, hand-polished finish.

MATERIALS NEEDED

unfinished wooden box—any size and
   shape
hand-carved wooden appliqués
very fine sandpaper
epoxy glue
tack rag
stain—in a wood color of your
   choice: walnut, oak, maple, etc.
clean cloth
steel wool—triple 0 grade
satin finish varnish
brush
turpentine
paste wax

DIRECTIONS

Sand the box and cover until both are perfectly smooth. Then wipe off all of the dust with a tack rag. The wooden appliqué should also be sanded if there are any rough edges.

With a clean cloth apply the stain, being sure to wipe off any excess. When the stain has dried, rub over the box with steel wool. Add another coat of stain and again rub lightly with steel wool.

Glue the appliqué to the cover of the box after the stain has dried. Pile

several books on top of the appliqué and let stand for 24 hours.

Give the box a coat of varnish, let it dry, and then rub with steel wool. Repeat the same procedure again, followed with four or five coats of paste wax.

Antique Bowl Table

What is it?
It starts as a bowl, but it ends as a

novel table for magazines or mail. Old bowls originally used to mix bread in are ideal. In any case, the bowl must be large, with a fairly flat bottom and sides which are at least an inch thick.

MATERIALS NEEDED

sandpaper—medium, fine and very fine grades
16-inch table legs—these come in a kit which includes the legs and brackets
wood stain—in any of the wood colors: walnut, oak, maple, etc.
satin finish varnish
clean cloth
paint brush
turpentine
steel wool—triple 0 grade
tack rag
paste wax
wooden bowl

DIRECTIONS

Remove the old finish from the bowl by sanding diligently with medium, fine and very fine sandpaper. If this doesn't do the trick, use a paint and varnish remover, following the manufacturer's instructions. When the bowl is completely sanded, go over it with a tack rag to remove all dust.

Sand the legs with fine and very fine sandpaper, and clean off dust.

Attach the leg brackets to the bottom of the bowl, following the directions on the kit, and screw the legs into place.

Then give the bowl and legs two coats of stain. This should be rubbed on with a clean cloth. Be sure to wipe off any excess.

When the stain is dry, rub over the entire table with steel wool and then a tack rag. Apply one coat of varnish, let it dry, and follow with steel wool. Add another coat of varnish, and finish with steel wool and two layers of paste wax.

Candleholders

Candlelight is extremely flattering —use it to your advantage!

Magnificently ornate candleholders can be made from an old banister or newel post, and give a dramatic effect wherever they are displayed.

MATERIALS NEEDED

parts of a banister—look for this at a wrecking, demolishing or salvage company
paint and varnish remover
putty knife
steel wool—triple 0 grade
sandpaper—medium, fine and very fine grades
saw
tack rag
paint brush
turpentine
Treasure Gold Wax Gilt (optional)
A device to hold the candle:
1. A bracket which may be screwed into the top of the candleholder, *or*
2. A bottle cover, painted and glued with epoxy glue to the top of the candleholder, *or*
3. A large nail pounded into the top of the candleholder with the head snipped off with wire cutters. (This will make a spike which can be pushed into the bottom of the candle)

DIRECTIONS

Strip the banister of the old finish by using a paint and varnish remover, following the manufacturer's directions.

Saw the banister in half to make two candleholders, and sand it until smooth, using various grades of sandpaper. Be sure to wipe off all dust with a tack rag when you're finished sanding.

Attach the device you've selected to hold the candle, and then paint, antique, or stain the candleholder. (See Chapter 8, page 118.)

When the paint is dry, Treasure Gold may be applied to emphasize various sections of the candleholder.

Mosaic Table

Hot coffee, burning cigarette ashes and bumps and bangs can't damage this durable table! Would you believe it's also pretty?

For versatility, you can't beat this artistic, comment-provoking table, which can be used advantageously with all furniture styles whether contemporary, traditional, modern or provincial.

MATERIALS NEEDED

½-inch mosaic tiles—you will need 3780 tiles. Don't let this figure stagger you! The tiles come attached to large sheets of paper backing, which makes them easy to handle. You may use one color or an assortment of colors

mosaic cement or glue

scraper and cement spreader

grout

¾-inch plywood—this will be the foundation for your table top, and should be 21 inches by 45 inches

molding—enough to go around the outside edge of the table

saw

rubber or plastic spoon or spatula

14-inch table legs—kit including brackets

flat or dull enamel—in a color of your choice

sponge
paper towels
paint brush
turpentine
hammer
small nails
sandpaper—fine and very fine grades

DIRECTIONS

Spread the cement on a small area of the plywood and firmly affix the tiles. Working in sections prevents the cement from drying too fast.

Continue applying cement and tile until the surface is completely covered. Let it dry for twenty-four hours.

Mix grout according to the directions on the package, and pour it on the table top. Spread it with a plastic spoon or spatula, and work it carefully into the cracks between each tile. When the grout has set for thirty minutes, use a damp sponge and paper towels to wipe the excess off the top of the tiles. Rub vigorously over the entire area, rinsing the sponge frequently. This will remove all grout except that which remains in the crevices. Dry for twenty-four hours.

Saw the molding to fit around the edges of the table, and nail in place.

Attach the legs.

Sand all wood, and paint with two coats of enamel.

Antique Duck Decoy

Here's an amusing, offbeat gift for the sportsman in your life.

A word of warning: Whatever you do, *don't* use his best hunting decoy! This can cause drastic repercussions.

MATERIALS NEEDED

duck decoy—made of cardboard or papier-mâché
semi-gloss enamel—any color can be used as the base coat
burnt umber oil paint
clean cloth
oil paints—three or four colors to be used for painting designs
paint brush
turpentine
semi-gloss varnish
Treasure Gold Wax Gilt

DIRECTIONS

Paint the decoy with two coats of enamel, letting it dry after each coat. Mix burnt umber with an equal amount of turpentine to make an antique glaze, and rub it on the duck with a cloth. Let it set for five minutes, and lightly wipe it off, leaving a trace of the burnt umber in grooves and indentations, and let it dry.

Draw whimsical flowers or designs on the duck with oil paints. This will probably take two days to dry completely.

Give your creation five coats of varnish to make it resemble china or porcelain. Then emphasize the bill, eyes and feathers with Treasure Gold.

Handmade Pottery

For thousands of years men have fashioned pottery from clay, and the art still holds a mysterious, enduring fascination.

All of us are born with an irrepressible urge to create. So why not yield to temptation, and express yourself in clay?

Whether these graceful pottery pieces are primitive, classical, or modern, they'll be unmistakably yours; and their characteristic simplicity is compatible with any decor.

MATERIALS NEEDED

moist self-hardening clay—this is the best type for the beginner to use, since objects made with this clay do not need to be fired in a kiln
heavy plastic bag—to store the clay
clean cloths
1 large piece of heavy plastic or oilcloth—to cover your work area. An old plastic tablecloth is ideal
pan of water
waterproof semi-gloss varnish
semi-gloss enamel—one color or several colors
paint brush
turpentine

DIRECTIONS

Cover your table with a piece of heavy plastic or oilcloth. This will give you a workable surface that the clay won't stick to, and it will also protect your table.

Here are several helpful pointers to remember when you are working with clay:

(1) Any clay you are not using should always be wrapped with a damp cloth and tightly enclosed in a plastic bag to keep it moist and workable.

(2) Should your clay become too dry, sprinkle a small amount of water

on it, and work the moisture into the clay by kneading it with your hands. Add just a little water at a time, so the clay becomes soft but not mushy.

(3) It's best to begin working with a small piece of clay. You can always take out more clay when you need it. If you start with too much, however, part of it may dry out.

Now you're ready to begin!

First, you must remove any air bubbles which may be in the clay. To do this, knead the clay vigorously for a few minutes. Then roll the clay into a ball, pick it up, and throw it forcefully onto the table. Repeat this procedure several times. This is very im-portant, because air pockets or bubbles will cause the pottery to crack when it dries.

The simplest way to make a piece of pottery is to use what is called the "coil method," but you may develop other techniques as you learn how to handle the clay.

To make a bowl using the "coil method," begin by patting and shaping a piece of clay into a round, flat shape—something like a thick pan-cake. This will be used as the base of the bowl.

Take another piece of clay, place it on the table, and roll it with the palms of your hands to form a long roll of clay about ½ inch in diameter.

BASE OF BOWL

SMOOTH SIDES

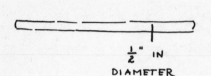

$\frac{1}{2}$" IN
DIAMETER

Then coil the roll of clay around the base, and continue winding coils, one on top of the other, until you have made the sides of the bowl.

Then put your bowl in a cool place to dry. To keep the pottery from drying too fast, which could result in cracking, lay a slightly dampened cloth over the bowl for the first day or so. Then remove the cloth to let it finish drying.

When the bowl is completely dry, paint it with enamel. Use one solid color or a pattern of various colors.

After the paint is dry, apply one coat of varnish. Let dry, and give it a second coat.

WIND COILS ONE
ON TOP OF OTHER

Blend the coils together to make the sides smooth by dipping your fingers in water, and rubbing them over the bowl, inside and out.

Individually Styled
Room Divider

Any merry monarch would delight in the charm and splendor of these dramatic and imaginative paneled screens.

Your home is your castle, so enhance and enrich it by relieving the monotony of the usual room divider made of wood, wrought iron or brick

with a screen designed to reflect your personal tastes and interests.

MATERIALS NEEDED

wooden frame only of a partitioned screen—these usually have three or four partitions or panels

heavy fabric—such as cotton, linen, burlap, sailcloth, brocade, moire taffeta, velvet or velveteen. Enough material to cover each partition, and allow for a 1-inch overlap on all sides

upholstery tacks—approximately four packages. If possible, choose a color to match or complement your fabric

hammer

scissors

measuring tape

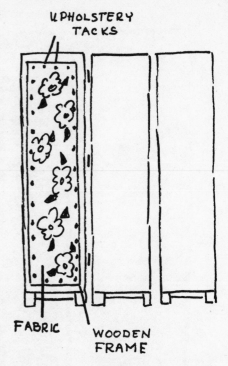

UPHOLSTERY TACKS

FABRIC   WOODEN FRAME

DIRECTIONS

Most screen frames can be bought already painted or stained. However, if yours is unfinished, this must be your first step. For directions, see Chapter 8.

Measure the length and width of one panel, and add 1 inch to your measurements. Cut one piece of material to these dimensions. Then place the screen flat on the floor, right side up, and lay the material evenly over the panel.

Work on one side at a time. Turn under a small hem, and use upholstery tacks to attach the material to the frame. The tacks should be evenly spaced, about 3 or 4 inches apart.

Now tackle another side, using the same method to attach the material to the frame, pulling the fabric slightly as you go to insure tautness.

The third and fourth sides of the panel are done in exactly the same

way. It is important to remember that *the material must be kept taut.*

Follow this procedure to cover the remaining panels.

Decorations may be attached to the panels and changed with the seasons and your changing whims.

Ice Tongs Candelabra

Have you succumbed to the lure of the Early American look? Are you an antiques enthusiast? Or is your

taste exclusively modern? If it's hard to imagine an article which manages to look ancient, rustic and modern at the same time, raise your gaze to the photograph above.

MATERIALS NEEDED

old-fashioned iron ice tongs—these may be a bit difficult to find. Try your attic, an antique store, or a junk shop

metal candleholding device—bracket for holding candles which may be glued to the ice tongs. (A metal bottle cover may also be used for this purpose)

liquid solder or epoxy glue

flat black spray enamel

candles

DIRECTIONS

Open the ice tongs to their full width, and place the handles of the tongs on the table. These will form the base of the candelabra.

To keep the tongs in this open position permanently, put liquid solder

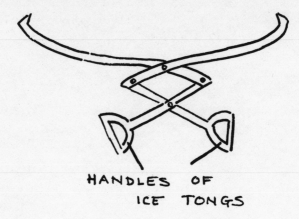

HANDLES OF
ICE TONGS

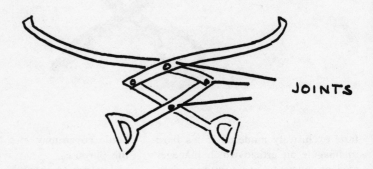

JOINTS

or epoxy glue in and around all of the joints. Use a toothpick to force the glue or solder into hard-to-reach spots.

When you are finished, let the solder or glue set until it becomes rigid. In humid weather, it is wise to wait a full day.

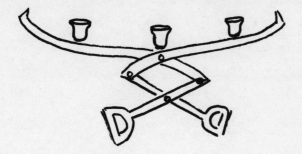

Next, attach three metal bottle covers or candleholding brackets to the top of the tongs, using liquid solder or epoxy glue to hold them in place.

Again let this set until hard, and then paint the entire candelabra with flat black spray enamel.

Insert your choice of candles after the paint has dried.

Epilogue

EPILOGUE

The male ego, when sufficiently aroused, is an awesome thing to behold. And believe me, your involvement with these projects will definitely arouse it! As a matter of fact, it may suffer slightly.

We all know that the average male considers himself a handyman around the house; a jack-of-all-trades, who is not only the breadwinner for the family, but who is also in his spare time an expert plumber, electrician, engineer, and master carpenter. Almost always he'd rather do things himself. This, of course, does NOT apply to cooking, cleaning, ironing, waxing, etc., which are by nature (?) women's work.

You may as well brace yourself. He wouldn't be human if he didn't resent (if only subconsciously) what he considers your trespass onto his masculine preserves.

Your first attempts at some of these projects will probably be received (at worst) with indulgent amusement, or (at best) with tolerant surprise.

If, after a few tries, you find you really enjoy the work and keep at it, you'll find that he will generally display a great deal of good-humored forbearance. He will also exhibit unmistakable signs of long-suffering neglect—especially if his dinner is sometimes delayed because you're tied up with one of your projects!

It's only natural that after a time he will offer occasional helpful suggestions. Who knows? He may even condescend to help you!

His attitude eventually will change to that of supreme unconcern. You will become all too familiar with that infuriatingly bland, typically masculine comment: "Hm. That's nice."

Finally, of course, he reaches the stage where he expresses indignant disbelief when you murmur that you "just can't possibly" do something or other. He has come to think of you as Mrs. Fixit—heaven forbid!

When this final stage has become apparent, it's high time to drop everything (at least temporarily) and dig out your most glamorous dress. Set the scene with flowers, wine and music—and his very favorite dinner. It'll require all of your feminine guile to change your image from "Mrs. Fixit" to "that wonderful girl I married."

On the other hand, if, after he's seen you with dirt on your nose, sawdust in your hair, sticky with glue and splattered with paint, wielding a saw and hammer with perfect aplomb, he STILL thinks you're as fragile as a butterfly, as feminine as Cleopatra, as seductive as Circe, and as helpless as a new-born kitten, please—write a book of your own and share your secret!